GOOD BOY
BAD BOY

GOOD BOY
BAD BOY

How to Stop Being Your Own Worst Enemy and Live
an Unapologetic Life of Joy, Success and Love

By Joel Primus with Shelley Singleton

Cover Design and typeset by Edge of Water Designs, edgeofwater.com
eBook production by Laura Kincaid, Ten Thousand | Editing + Book Design, www.tenthousand.co.uk

ISBNs:
978-1-0688891-0-3 (Paperback)
978-1-0688891-2-7 (Hardcover)
978-1-0688891-1-0 (eBook)
978-1-0688891-3-4 (Audiobook)

DEKAN Publishing
Vancouver, BC, Canada

Dedication

For my daughters Quinn, Romyn and Jovi

Acknowledgements

I would like to thank my wife for supporting the time and space needed to write this book and continue the journey of personal growth and healing. I would like to thank my mother and father for their life-long dedication to 'healing the line' and my co-author Shelley for her endless enthusiasm, creativity, wisdom and patience.

Table of Contents

Introduction 13

Chapter 1 — Duality 23

Chapter 2 — Beginnings 31

Chapter 3 — Voices..39

Chapter 4 — Belonging 51

Chapter 5 — Unconscious...61

Chapter 6 — Perception 71

Chapter 7 — Permission..87

Chapter 8 — Emotion 97

Chapter 9 — Forgiveness 111

Chapter 10 — Harmony 123

Chapter 11 — Freedom 133

Bibliography... 145

About The Author 153

Other Works By Joel Primus.. 155

"What is a good man but a bad man's teacher?
What is a bad man but a good man's job?"

~ Lao Tzu

Introduction

Everything that we see is a shadow cast by that which we do not see.

~ Martin Luther King Jr.

Some 8,000 years ago, mirrors made from polished obsidian were used in Turkey and Egypt to reflect a person's appearance. By the 17th and 18th centuries in Europe, mirrors were also used for dispersing additional light, as well as for creating a greater sense of spaciousness. Today, the mirror has become an essential tool for self-monitoring, hanging over the sink in virtually every bathroom.

So, when you look in the mirror, who do you see?

Do you see someone who has persevered through challenges and learned lessons that have made them stronger and more well-rounded as a human being? Do you see someone who is proud of their uniqueness and of what they contribute to the world? Do you see a physical body that is almost miraculous for how it functions? Is the person staring back at you worthy of praise, joy, success, and love?

Do you see a *good* person?

Or do you see the toll that a series of mistakes and failures has taken? A person who is not as good as their friends and peers? Someone who is flawed and imperfect and worthy of harsh judgement? Do your shoulders sag with regret, shame, or guilt? Do you feel the person staring back at you needs to work harder and achieve more to be worthy of praise, joy, success, and love?

Do you see a *bad* person?

Maybe you see both.

At age fourteen, when I looked into the mirror, I saw only a bad person. No matter how much I accomplished or who I pleased, my life was pervaded by an unshakeable, underlying *feeling* of badness.

This feeling of badness grew to consume me. It pushed me to make choices based on what I thought others wanted me to do, or what I *thought* was good, or what I *thought* I should do, regardless of how I felt inside. But none of that resulted in the love and acceptance that I truly sought. Doing what I thought was the "right" thing just led to deeper feelings of unworthiness. No matter what I did, I was never good enough.

Perhaps you've felt the same? For so long, I thought this affliction was exclusively mine, which only made the feelings worse; later I learned I was not alone. According to Swiss psychiatrist Carl Jung, "Unfortunately, there can be no doubt that man is, on the whole, less good than he imagines himself or wants to be. Everyone carries a shadow, and the less it is embodied in the individual's conscious life, the blacker and denser it is."

Of course, I didn't know it when I was a teenager, but that moment, in front of that mirror I met my shadow. The *shadow self* is a term Jung coined to describe the aspects of our personality we don't like and therefore reject; it's our "badness." It is the counterpoint to what he called the persona or conscious ego.

The shadow is the side of our personality that resides in the metaphorical darkness. We hide it and repress it and feel laden with guilt for harboring this shadow because, in part, it contains the emotions and impulses we've learned to consider negative: lust, greed, power, anger, envy, and more. It's the part of ourselves we would rather not acknowledge or allow to be seen. But the more we repress our shadow self, the more powerful and malevolent it becomes. As a teenager, whizzing through life, I unconsciously kept pushing more and more of myself into the shadow.

"If an inferiority is conscious, one always has a chance to correct it," Jung said. "Furthermore, it is constantly in contact with other interests, so that it is continually subjected to modifications. But if it is repressed and isolated from consciousness, it never gets corrected." Meaning, if we are aware that our sense of inferiority is limiting us, we can change our behavior.

The cues we receive about what is good and bad are all around us. Society, media, religion, teachers, and our parents relentlessly voice the message: some behaviors are good, others are bad; some emotions are good, others are bad. And no one wants to be around a bad person. But when the external messages we receive conflict with how we feel, inner turmoil can result. And within this turmoil lives anxiety, shame, guilt, judgement, and feelings of unworthiness. Such inner conflict limits what we believe is possible and holds us back from a fulfilling life.

This dichotomy between good and bad—our perception of being good or being bad—is what we'll explore in this book because, contrary to what we have been taught, these two concepts are not polar opposites. Nor are they mutually exclusive. In fact, only by embracing both the good and bad within ourselves, in others, and in the world can we free ourselves from the limiting beliefs that deny us joy, success, and love. That holistic integration of our shadow self into our consciousness signifies true maturity where, ultimately, we can come to understand that are we neither good nor bad, we just *are*.

When I was young, I took up long-distance running. I became obsessed with keeping a daily log to track my progress. This log eventually morphed into a journal where I spilled deeper thoughts, fears, and questions onto the pages. Long before I could have a meaningful dialogue with my inner self, I was curious about this inner self, but in a biased way—like a child tattling on a sibling, unaware of their own role in creating the displeasing situation. I wanted to understand what was going on inside so I could make sense of myself and the world, but I bumbled along for quite some time before I became more aware of what was happening inside me, and things finally started to click.

Through the years, I'd periodically head to the garage, dust off the box labeled *Joel's Stuff*, and flip through those old journals. Worry and angst were common themes for the younger me, but the biggest throughline was my longing to understand why I felt *bad* about so many things, especially given how *good* I appeared to have it. No answers came right away, but I kept asking.

According to the American Psychological Association, dichotomous thinking can be defined as "the tendency to think in terms of polar opposites—that is, in terms of the best and worst—without accepting the possibilities that lie between these two extremes." My younger self, not knowing any better, constantly classified things as right or wrong, good or bad and couldn't see past the dichotomy to a compassionate self-view devoid of judgement.

We humans are complex, nuanced creatures who live in the messy middle of life, a hard and confusing place where it is difficult to reconcile the goodness of our hearts with the chaos of our minds.

No question about it, finding inner peace and happiness as a human is a constant struggle.

Part of the reason I feel compelled to write this book now is because a healthy appreciation and understanding of that nuanced struggle between good and bad is in short supply these days, just as it was for me when I was a kid. In some ways, nuance is the fine thread that sews our differences together. Nuance is vital for compassion, tolerance, acceptance, and progress to manifest in this complex and rapidly changing world, a world in which fear is wielded as a weapon to keep us in a pattern of dependence on institutions and to suppress our potential for growth, self-acceptance, and self-awareness.

While fear manifests in almost every facet of life, I personally became aware of it in 2016.

I was watching the TV news in my tiny apartment outside New York City, when a headline stopped me short: *The Year of Fear*. It appeared on the banner at the bottom of the screen. A warning signal shot from my gut to my brain and was amplified by the talking heads as they discussed the acts of terrorism that were being perpetrated around the world.

This stark presentation of fear in the form of violence and distrust conflicted with how I saw the world. Whatever my inner struggles were, I believed the world to be a welcoming and safe place, a good place, with good people. In the past, I had explored many so-called dangerous places, from Honduras to Lebanon to Cambodia, and had left each with memories of people's kindness, generosity, and incredible hospitality. Even at home in Canada, I had pushed the boundaries of safety by sticking out my thumb and hitchhiking from one coast to the other. Kindness and generosity had accompanied me once again.

The fear narrative spewing from the TV was jarring—there was no balance or nuance in the reporting. In Canada they talked about murderous hitchhikers abroad. They portrayed terrorist events as if every person in the rogue country was guilty of the same crime. Over time, the villainization of people, places, and groups has been magnified. The media now proclaims, "We will tell you what is bad and who is bad!" This isn't new, of course. External influencing and shaping of perceptions have happened throughout history, but after I first noticed the manipulation for what it was, the floodgates opened wide.

Was it just a narrative of current events that shaped our perspectives of the world around us, or was it also shaping how we felt about ourselves?

I wondered why it seemed like society, as reflected in the media and institutions, was so hellbent on casting a dark cloud over our lives, shifting us towards judgement and fear. I wanted to uncover why this was happening and how we could overcome it. But not just for me; I had an instinctual need to show my young daughters that the true spirit of the world was not reflected by the media or even by society at large. My girls would need to get out there and see things for themselves. They would have to gather their own evidence and form their own opinions instead of adopting those the media, politicians, corporations, and, yes, even their parents pushed on them.

If they could see discrepancies between what was being said about people and events in the wider world versus their own lived experiences, maybe they could also recognize discrepancies and nuance within themselves, as well as understand that external influences were shaping much of what they learned to accept as true.

So, in 2018 my wife and I sold our Jeep, packed our bags, and took our two girls (then aged two and six) on a journey around the globe. I wanted them to see firsthand what I had experienced in my travels: we live in a world of grey where good and bad are held in a delicate balance.

As we roamed from the Middle East to South America and then around the edges of the Arctic Circle, we witnessed a lot of hardship and suffering. But right alongside that we saw courage, generosity, love, divergent opinions based on shared values, and the unshakable human spirit. I wanted my girls to see and acknowledge the existence of both, and to be thankful for the beauty of the shared human experience.

When we touched down at home after the last leg of our trip, I was even more troubled by what I was seeing, despite arriving in the same place we'd left.

Reverse culture shock can happen when you return to a familiar place that feels uncomfortably different from when you left, different because you've adapted to foreign places and now see home from a different perspective. Sometimes home actually *is* different. Re-adjusting can be plagued with confusion, loneliness, and disconnection.

We'd been catapulted back into a culture of mass hysteria, divisiveness, and negativity. Fear and the badness of the "other" felt like a juggernaut that had ripped through the fabric of society, and in a way I hadn't experienced before. The perception of a dangerous world fueled a collective anxiety, and this anxiety was further exacerbated by social media and mass media.

The indomitable human spirit that once underpinned our thriving Western society was, it seemed to me, disappearing. What happened to the civil disagreements that built our democracies? Differing viewpoints were fracturing into niche offerings; algorithms enabled viewers to exclusively enjoy opinions that reinforced their own. This curation of information, with different ideologies pushed into diametrical opposition, tickled our primal brains, and we were once again angry tribes at war with each other.

My family had arrived home to a feast of the not-so-tasty Crab Mentality, or the Theory Crabs, which is most simply defined as "If I can't have it, neither can you." Schadenfreude, defined as the pleasure derived from the misery or misfortune of others, was on full display. I watched this tempest of fear and anger grow, and it became clear that it was fed, at least in part, by how we each felt about ourselves. People were starring as the victim in stories about themselves and their tribe.

Are we about to permanently lose sight of the goodness in the world and in others because of an inability to recognize it in ourselves? Why is society's shadow so prominent? Is this an opportunity to integrate our shadow selves individually, which will subsequently impact the broader community? In my experience, the worse I feel inside—unworthy, undeserving, not good enough, like I don't belong—the more addictive the media machine becomes. This is because it feeds my need to fixate on the external bad in the world so that I can avoid confronting the bad I feel inside. This creates a self-sustaining cycle of negativity.

I knew I had to do my best to break this cycle for me and for my family. I had spent a good chunk of my life struggling to feel "good" and be "good" while feeling like a perpetual failure, always a bad boy inside. I certainly did not want to unconsciously pass this mentality on to my children; instead, I wanted my family to benefit from the learning I was endeavoring to acquire. We can help heal our next of kin with what my wife calls, healing the line. Some even believe the radius of our individual healing extends beyond our inner circle of spouse and children, reaching back to our parents and grandparents, and laterally to our friends and extended family. We can do this by healing ourselves.

Taking personal accountability sounded like the only strategy to me, and so I committed to deepening my own healing as a parent, son, husband, and friend. When we heal our own traumas, we change how we act, respond, and speak, thereby breaking the pattern of inflicting our wounds on our children or perpetuating the wounds of our parents. The traumas we address need not be horrific, life-altering events.

Each trauma with a little *t* is like a snowflake. Each one may be innocuous on its own, but they can accumulate over the years and bury us. At ski resorts they trigger mini avalanches throughout the season to reduce the risk of a giant, destructive one building up. We can do the same thing; instead of letting emotions collect and build, we can process them as they come up.

Life experiences, including traumatic ones, shape our mindset, our perspective, as well as the stories we tell ourselves about good and bad. We're wired to denote and categorize our interpretations of events. Our brains do not register absolute truths, only our interpretations, and so faulty interpretations can rob us of feeling good, feeling loved, and feeling accepted.

I am not a moral authority on good and bad. What I present here is open to interpretation, and I approach this topic primarily from shadow work, which entails investigating and integrating the unconscious aspects of oneself, such as repressed emotions, fears, and desires as well as from intentional and unintentional societal conditioning. It's a chance to look within to find your truth. It is a reminder of your inherent goodness, but also an acknowledgement that skewed interpretations of information and events throughout your life can limit your perception of what's possible, affecting how you live and present yourself in the world.

The first part of this book focuses on the roots of the problem, showing how we got here. The second part of the book offers the solutions I've discovered through my experiences.

From now on, when you look in the mirror, my hope is that you can hold the ideas of both good and bad simultaneously and see yourself as the multi-dimensional, nuanced, mature human being you are. And, most importantly, to let your inherent goodness shine through.

1

Duality

An old Cherokee is teaching his grandson about life:

> *"A fight is going on inside me," he says to the boy, tapping his chest. "It is a terrible fight, and it is between two wolves. One is evil—he is anger, envy, sorrow, regret, greed, arrogance, self-pity, guilt, resentment, inferiority, lies, false pride, superiority, and ego."*

> *He continues, "The other is good—he is joy, peace, love, hope, serenity, humility, kindness, benevolence, empathy, generosity, truth, compassion, and faith. The same fight is going on inside you," he says, laying a hand on the boy's heart, "and inside every other person, too."*

> *The boy thinks about it for a minute and then asks his grandfather, "Which wolf will win?"*

> *The old Cherokee simply replies, "The one you feed.*

As adults we tend to overcomplicate things. I am constantly surprised by my daughters' wisdom in how they see the world. Because they are so young and haven't been exposed to many negative messages, they rely on their internal wisdom, and I want them to preserve that instinct for as long as possible. One of my most important roles as a father is to help my girls navigate good and bad, both externally and internally, so they don't grab for one while releasing the other. I want them to know their inner wolves and to know that it's okay to keep following their intuition and curiosity regardless of what anyone else (including me) thinks. This type of integration of all aspects of the self is part of becoming a whole, mature human, one who is capable of extending empathy and compassion to themselves and others.

I don't want them to worry about the inevitable slip-ups they'll make while following their internal wisdom. At the same time, it is not my role as a parent to protect them from mistakes. Their own growth and healing will determine which ones they make, and when. But, like any parent, I hold dear a morsel of hope that I can lead by example, empowering them to shake off their perceived limitations and failings. Dad wisdom carries weight for at least a little while, right?

Now that my first two daughters are a little older and have some experiences tucked under their belts, when they do struggle, I share a parable, fable, or story to deliver lessons in their simplest form. A rational explanation may fly high over their heads, but they can relate to a well-told story. Wisdom tales help all of us recognize what's happening inside our minds and bodies so we can look within to find our truth. Each time we hear a simple story that teaches a profound truth, it gives us an opportunity to learn something new.

The origin of the tale that starts this chapter is said to be unknown, but it's often attributed to the Cherokee tribe. Through the years, the story has been given many titles. One of them is *The Wolves Within*. This title strikes a personal chord because it encapsulates the conflict in the duality of good and bad that disturbs our inner sense of wholeness.

John Locke, the seventeenth-century English philosopher, argued that knowledge is only acquired through sensory experiences. He proposed the idea that at birth the mind is a blank slate, or *tabula rasa* in Latin. As we go through life, that slate is filled with ideas and experiences. Locke is recognized as one of the first great empiricists because he theorized that all knowledge is derived from empirical observation and sensory experience.

Tabula rasa is used in the epistemology branch of philosophy that ponders the theory of knowledge as well as in psychology to underscore how impactful the external world is and how it shapes us as individuals. The idea is that we emerge from the womb pure and untainted. Then life happens, and all those experiences shape how we act—good and bad—and how we see ourselves. Classic nature versus nurture.

But there's another perspective. In his book *Just Babies: The Origins of Good and Evil*, Yale psychology professor Paul Bloom suggests babies are born with a sense of morality—they are not blank slates at all. He demonstrates through research that babies are able to judge the goodness and badness of others' actions.

Both schools of thought do concede, however, that our experiences play a huge role in how we see ourselves and interpret the world. This means we have some control over what we perceive as good and bad, even if it's unconscious. By becoming aware of our perceptions, we can dissect them, challenge them, and change them. We can choose which wolf to feed.

Children are both blessed and burdened with inherited spoonfuls of their parents' perceptions of the world. It's natural for a parent to want to pass along wisdom and personal views from the lessons they've learned to save their children the pain of making the same mistakes; however, if as parents we haven't yet learned from our own missteps then we're just perpetuating them with our dear children. I'm again reminded of the pessimistic wisdom of John Locke: "Parents wonder why the streams are bitter, when they themselves poison the fountain."

As described above, beyond just our parents, the outer world has an outsized impact on us. Society, religion, and other external influences shape our behavior. We hear messages like, "It's the right thing to do," "Because I said so," "That's what Jesus would do," "You don't want to upset your father, do you?" "I wouldn't do that if I were you!" and many, many more warnings meant to keep us on a safe path. But are these subtle messages doing us a disservice? Are we receiving mixed messages about what society feels about those actions versus how *we* feel, forcing us into dichotomous thinking where we feel obliged to favor the external message?

Here are two straightforward examples.

You enjoy playing in the dirt, but you're told you're bad for getting your new shoes muddy.

Or maybe you feel all that lovely and delicious oxytocin from kissing your crush after school, but the jealous neighbor kid saw you, told his parents who told your parents, and you were punished for doing something "adult."

These experiences can all feed our shadow the "bad" virus, which differs from our lived experience of feeling free and joyful. Of course, kids need rules. But without context or explanation for what the crime is (if there even *is* one), we struggle to reconcile the negative external message with the internal joy in the moment.

Here's another example for you.

I knew someone in middle school, let's call her Sam, who was quite thin. You'd think that was a good thing because modern society values slender body types and thin people have fewer health risks. But "You're so skinny! Don't you ever eat?" played on repeat throughout her middle and high school years. Sam was called a stick figure, and kids asked if she was anorexic. One day a schoolmate shoved a cupcake in her face, saying, "Here, you need this more than I do."

From her family and other adults, she constantly heard, "You'll be happy when you're older," which subtly suggested that her body wasn't acceptable then but would be later. She learned that happiness is tied to the way you look—a message we've all heard repeatedly in some form or another.

Is being thin good or bad? For Sam, the negative comments outnumbered the positive ones, leading her to feel self-conscious and have low self-esteem. The overarching message of "you're not good enough the way you are" stayed with her long after she grew up and filled out.

These are all confusing messages we experience as children and adolescents, messages that can result in conflating felt emotions and otherwise innocent life experiences with other, often negative and judgmental reactions.

Growing up with endless contradictions is confusing because the external world seems at odds with our own experience; what's more it is detrimental to feeling secure as our *own* self.

In the book *And Then They Stopped Talking to Me: Making Sense of Middle School*, author Judith Warner describes the middle school feeling as one of "excruciating awkwardness, painful self-consciousness, and crippling insecurity in the face of harsh and unforgiving peer judgment; a sense of being alone, on the outside, and unacceptable."

Biology is partly to blame, according to Warner. "Scientists now speak of the middle school passage as a 'second critical period'—a stage of rapid brain changes and also of cognitive, behavioral, and social development that rivals in consequence the much-better-recognized 0–3 age range."

She also asserts that our narrative identity is impacted by what we suffered during those tween years. Narrative identity is "a person's internalized and evolving life story, integrating the reconstructed past and imagined future to provide life with some degree of unity and purpose."

In other words, who we become is greatly affected by what we agonized through in middle school, and because our brains at that time were still developing, our sense of self can be confused and contorted like your school drama teacher trying to have you (and the class) act out her inspired interpretation of the newest Cirque Du Soleil.

Sam wouldn't have believed there was anything wrong with her if not for the teasing she endured and the messages she received about acceptable body types. Internally, she didn't feel her weight was a problem, creating a disconnect between her internal and external worlds.

Cognitive dissonance—the mental discomfort resulting from holding two conflicting beliefs, values, attitudes, or behaviors simultaneously—can occur when external messages don't match internal feelings. When we don't *feel* bad or wrong, but we're told we're bad or unacceptable, we try to resolve the disconnect to relieve the discomfort. Often that means accepting the external message as truth and quieting or dismissing the internal.

These may seem like small and overly simplified examples but think of the hundreds of thousands of micro messages we receive throughout our lives that don't match our felt experience or our inner truth.

By taking on the aspects of what we hear, we stop trusting our judgement of what is true and good for ourselves. After a while this goes on autopilot, so our new instinct is to follow what others say or do instead of how we actually feel, all so we can fit in. Next thing we know, we've overfed the wrong wolf.

Then, the part of ourselves we stop listening to becomes a shameful, unwanted fragment. This is the shadow self. Whereas its opposite, the ego, represents the conscious mind, where our thoughts live, the shadow is the part of ourselves we want to hide. We view it as bad, evil, shameful, unfit to see the light of day.

Many of us treat our shadow like an irksome college roommate who is always pointing out what we do wrong or what we shouldn't be doing at all, and generally bugging the shit out of us. Someone we desperately want to get rid of but can't (at least until the next semester) so we do everything in our power to ignore them.

As we go through life ignoring our feelings because we no longer trust them, our shadow grows. It tells us what we're doing isn't good enough, and it tells us *we're* not good enough. It tells us we're unlovable. It tells us we're bad.

The shadow also gobbles up joyful aspects of ourselves that we are conditioned to disown. Growing up I loved to play in the swamp behind our house and pretend I was an explorer. When my mom rang the dinner bell (figuratively, of course—I didn't grow up in 1915), I ignored it. Do you think I was rewarded for coming home late, smelling like rotten fish and sewage? Of course not. Moreover, my parents and teachers thought a bright future was bestowed upon those who turned in their homework on time, not those engaged in "adventuring and exploring." Why it couldn't be both, I don't know.

In this way a duality is formed within us. We double down on what is good, while desperately repressing what is deemed bad.

As for me, eventually I fell in line and became the arbiter of respectable timeliness, discipline, and good ol' authoritative priorities.

Perhaps some version of this happened to you, too, where you exchanged your creative and wild spirit for something more practical and productive. Maybe now the issue is coming back to roost in your life, like it did for me.

We ignore our shadow because we've been conditioned to, but where and when did the sun of our life cast this shadow? Where did all things "bad" actually begin?

2

Beginnings

God did say, 'You must not eat fruit from the tree that is in the middle of the garden, and you must not touch it, or you will die.

For God knows that when you eat from it your eyes will be opened, and you will be like God, knowing good and evil.

When the woman saw that the fruit of the tree was good for food and pleasing to the eye, and also desirable for gaining wisdom, she took some and ate it. She also gave some to her husband, who was with her, and he ate it.

Then the man and his wife heard the sound of the Lord God as he was walking in the garden in the cool of the day, and they hid from the Lord God among the trees of the garden.

And the Lord God said, "The man has now become like one of us, knowing good and evil. He must not be allowed to reach out his hand and take also from the tree of life and eat, and live forever.

So, the Lord God banished him from the Garden of Eden to work the ground from which he had been taken.

~ Genesis 3 (NIV)

Human beings' attempt to reconcile with a moral path is shaped through an oral and written history that is both literal and parabolic. We know these teachings as mythology and religion and they paint the tapestry of our human existence in the polarity of good and bad.

Today, roughly 85 percent of people on this planet identify with a religion, and Christianity is the most popular, with a whopping 2.4 billion followers. I was among those followers.

Growing up attending church, however, was not my thing. It meant putting on uncomfortable clothes and sitting still for a full hour. And at lunch following the service, my parents would usually adopt some new house rule based on the sermon, a rule that I'd have to follow from then on.

When I wasn't fidgeting in the overly incensed air of the sacred sanctuary, I'd be down in the musty Sunday school basement. A slight improvement, but not by much. I would have rather been playing outside in my swamp, thank you very much.

Despite my lack of attention, religion provided much of my foundation for understanding good and bad, as it does for many people. The Bible is chock-full of lessons about how to walk a righteous path and avoid the pitfalls of evil, or else receive punishment. Under the inevitable rules my parents concocted, my role was to simply listen and obey. But even back then I felt a tinge of rebellion brewing. I yearned to push boundaries placed around me. I wanted to eat that fruit and go find forbidden and dangerous obstacles to test myself against. The parenting lexicon of "no," "can't," or "shouldn't" only ignited my fires of curiosity and sense of wonder. On the other hand, complying to stay safe and be a good boy didn't always feel right inside.

According to the ancient Jewish history, Josephus Methuselah (himself an ancient historian) recorded the history of the world as told by Adam onto stone obelisks that were carried by Noah on the ark and deposited in Arabia Moses was directed by God to seek out these obelisks and thus learn the history of the world.

This history is overflowing with tales of the fight between good and bad. The dichotomy is portrayed in the Bible as epic battles between friend and foe, hero and villain. The Bible tells of the triumph of good over evil. These tales serve as a metaphor for our individual inner journey through life—how to feed the wolves within us—where we must set out on an adventure (life), overcome obstacles (evil), then return transformed (goodness).

This is what twentieth-century American writer and professor Joseph Campbell called the monomyth, or Hero's Journey. It's a concept based on mythology that outlines the journey of an archetypical hero. According to Campbell, "A hero ventures forth from the world of common day into a region of supernatural wonder: fabulous forces are there encountered, and a decisive victory is won: the hero comes back from this mysterious adventure with the power to bestow boons on his fellow man."

This reminds me of how we can heal our family line when we start with healing ourselves.

George Lucas credited Campbell's book *The Hero with a Thousand Faces* as a major influence on his writing of the Star Wars sagas. And Christopher Vogler, a Hollywood executive, used Campbell's Hero's Journey framework to write his screenwriting guide *The Writer's Journey: Mythic Structure for Writers.*

Stories help us learn by providing vicarious sensory experiences that etch perceptions on our blank slate.

If you turn on the television, go to the movies, or flip open a book, the Hero's Journey is everywhere: *The Odyssey, The Wizard of Oz, The Matrix, Shrek,* and the Harry Potter series. Why is it so prevalent? Not because we imagine ourselves as heroes in our own lives, slaying metaphorical dragons and emerging triumphant, but because we *are* those heroes. The Hero's Journey represents our epic search for meaning in this world.

Yet, paradoxically, we often cast ourselves as the villain, believing we are bad, or at least not good enough.

Going back about two thousand years, you can see this play out in the *Bhagavad Gita*, a seven-hundred-verse Hindu scripture that is sometimes referred to as the Hindu Bible or *Song of the Lord*. You can read the whole thing in an hour, but I'll summarize it here:

On an ancient field of battle, two great armies line up across from one another. Chariots, horses, swords, armor. The invincible warrior, Arjuna, stands in formation on one side. He's our hero. Arjuna peers across at the enemy—he's close enough to see their faces. He recognizes people he knows. In great distress, he orders his charioteer to drive out to the space between the two armies and to stop. His charioteer obeys. There, Arjuna lays down his arms and refuses to fight.

"I see friends, kinsmen, teachers across the enemy line. Nothing good can come from contending against them or slaying them." He relinquishes his immortal bow, Gandiva, and slumps against his chariot in despair.

But here's the brilliant twist. Arjuna's charioteer is Krishna, the Supreme

God, one of the most revered of all Indian deities. Krishna stands before Arjuna and reads him the riot act: "You are a warrior! Stand up and fight!"

But wait. The names of the enemy warriors can be translated from Sanskrit to read as qualities of human vices, mortal failings common to us all. The list of names reads like this:

Fear

Ignorance

Complacency

Self-doubt

Disrespect for others

Impatience

Guilt

The *Gita* is talking about the inner war. When Krishna commands Arjuna to slay these enemies, he is asking him to defeat the vices inside Arjuna's own heart. Krishna then declares the reason these vices are evil is because they separate the mortal soul from uniting with the Almighty. They pull Arjuna away from Krishna.

The outer war in the *Gita* becomes a metaphor for the war within. A proposition that is both literally and parabolically contained in many religious teachings. American journalist and author Richard Heinberg points out: "Every religion begins with the recognition that human consciousness has been separated from the divine Source, that a former sense of oneness… has been lost…everywhere in religion and myth there is an acknowledgment that we have departed from an original…innocence and can return to it only through the resolution of some profound inner discord…the cause of the Fall is described variously as disobedience, as the eating of a forbidden fruit [from the tree of knowledge], and as spiritual amnesia [forgetting, blocking out, alienation/psychosis]."

Through religion we learn how to be good, how to avoid evil, and how to be closer to God. And we do this by conquering the vices that supposedly separate us. These ancient texts allow for free will and support free will but warn that when we follow temptation or disobey God, there are consequences. An eternity burning in hell being the main one! Certainly not on the top of anyone's bucket list.

Yet, as a wee little Sunday schooler, hell is a place I was told I'd go more times than I can count. A place that, even if you're not practicing a religion that acknowledges the existence of the binary heaven and hell, can still create a parental quagmire.

Child to parent: Some kid at school today told me that if I don't listen to the teacher, I'm going to hell. Is hell real, Mom?

Parent to self: If I tell my child there is no such thing as hell, they will tell the kid at school and that kid will tell their parents and after-school pick up will be awkward. If I do tell my kid some people believe hell is real, they'll probably turn all the actions of their life into Santa Claus' naughty and nice list and worry themselves sick. Alternatively, I could explain my new age spirituality about heaven and hell, but I'm still trying to figure that out myself, so I'll probably just confuse them.

I'm not aiming to make a caricature of religion here. To the contrary, I find the lessons of religion more and more interesting and meaningful the older I get. No, I only share this example to elucidate that whether it's 3000 B.C. or 2024, the conversation around good and bad is one we'll never uniformly agree on. More on that later.

Back to religion …

According to Judaism, every human has two inclinations: the *yetzer hatov* (good) and the *yetzer hara* (evil). We all have tendencies toward both, but we have the power to resist the bad and choose the good. *Yetzer hara* shows up in Genesis 8:21: "The imagination of the heart of man is evil from his youth." It is believed we are born with a desire to seek pleasure, property, security, and so forth. If left to run rampant, this tendency can lead to greed, gluttony, perversion, and other sins, but by following the word of God, we can keep it in check.

Then, of course, there is karma, a belief found in Hinduism, Sikhism, Buddhism, Jainism, and Ayyavazhi. Karma describes a complex cosmic law of cause and effect that is a fundamental part of existence. Believing actions have consequences, people feel a sense of responsibility in how they live their lives and how they treat others. The details of how karma plays out vary according to religion, with some tying karma to reincarnation and the message, basically explained as: Act positively and you will be reborn into a happy life; act negatively and that rebirth won't be much fun.

Lessons about good and bad are as ancient as we are, and they are the beginnings of what helps to form our moral compass. They are also at the beginnings of how humans began to make sense of, and interact with, our human experience on earth. But some of what was intended to protect us also ended up harming us.

Religion, ancient tales, and heroic stories certainly aren't the only sources of information we receive about good and bad.

These spiritual and religious traditions may provide the promised path of salvation, oneness and enlightenment, but when do they become confusing voices in our head?

In modern times, plenty of external voices compete for our attention and inform how we think about our own goodness and badness. And, as we discussed in the first chapter, when we're kids with developing brains, we can't always discern what information is helpful and what ends up holding us back later. We're simply taught to listen to our elders and respect authority.

3

Voices

*We are born with the capacity to learn how to dream, and the humans
who live before us teach us how to dream the way society dreams.
The outside dream has so many rules that when a new human is born,
we hook the child's attention and introduce these rules into his
or her mind. The outside dream uses Mom and Dad, the schools,
and religion to teach us how to dream.*

~ Don Miguel Ruiz, "The Four Agreements: A Practical Guide
to Personal Freedom"

One night when I was putting my daughters to bed, one of them said, "Daddy, I want to get my ears pierced. When can you take me?" She was six years old.

A bit taken aback, I said, "I'll take you, but you know it hurts, right?"

"Yeah, I know," she said, totally unfazed.

My eldest daughter, on the bunk bed below, muttered to herself but loud enough for us to hear, "Great. My younger sister is brave enough to get her ears pierced, and so are my friends, but I'm not."

My first instinct was to turn to my older daughter and tell her that she *was* brave enough to get her ears pierced too. But I caught myself. Her bravery did not lie in doing what her younger sister wanted to do but in trusting her gut, which was telling her she wasn't ready. Following her own timing instead of caving to the pressure of others was the definition of brave, especially at her age.

I had a choice: I could double down on the message society was telling her about bravery and how her fear of getting her ears pierced placed her outside of that category, or I could reaffirm her internal truth about not being ready, even though her younger sister was.

My attempt at explaining this came out in some dad-like jumbled concoction that leaned heavily on the character Merida from the Disney movie *Brave*. I have the Merida stuffy sitting on the bed to thank for that little burst of inspiration. In the movie, Merida is called brave for defying her parents' expectations and following her own path. If Cinderella had been sitting there instead, the conversation may have gone in a totally different direction.

After leaving the room, I thought about how close I had come to betraying my daughter's bravery by saying something pithy like, "You can be brave like your sister." How many times had I blundered before, accidentally comparing her to someone else or discounting and invalidating her true feelings? How many times did she feel she wasn't good enough because of something I said?

That initial knee-jerk reaction, chock-full of my own shame and judgement, was based on what I had heard and experienced in so many different ways growing up. My parents had told me I was a good kid. I'm sure in their hearts they felt I was good because I was their child and they loved me, but that's not how I heard it. I believed I was good because I was helpful and usually compliant. Good because I won a school competition, and teachers liked me.

Good because I became an athlete who won races and championships and scholarships. Good because newspapers wrote about me and opportunities came my way. I was good because of what I did, not because of who I was.

I thought being a good kid meant obeying adults and doing what they expected of me (being brave included), regardless of how I felt. I realized that if I wasn't conscious of it, I would project those collective experiences onto my daughters.

In fact, projecting behaviors we're conscious of may only be one part of the trauma our children inherit from us.
Enter epigenetics. A fancy word that sounds like something I picked up from the paleobiologist in Jurassic Park but is actually the study of how our environment and other factors can change the way our genes are expressed. Yep, according to epigenetics, external events can actually affect our biology. They don't change our genes per se, but they can change how those genes are expressed when passed down. Moreover, epigenetic changes can influence development, mental health, and trauma.

While epigenetics is still an emerging field, the number of studies has grown in recent years. One such study referenced in a BBC article looked at US Civil War POWs whose sons and grandsons suffered higher rates of mortality than the wider population. Even more interesting, children born to these men before they became prisoners of war didn't show that same spike in mortality; only sons born after their father's POW camp experience did.

According to BBC journalist Martha Henriques, "Wars, famines and genocides are all thought to have left an epigenetic mark on the descendants of those who suffered them."

It's incredible to think the trauma of our parents and grandparents can be passed down. The good news is these studies also suggest inherited trauma can be undone with techniques like cognitive behavioral therapy. So, we *can* actually heal the line. By healing ourselves we pass that gift onto our kids in more ways than one.

That night I tossed and turned knowing I couldn't undo all the times I'd failed to honor each of the girls' feelings and choices, projecting my views onto them instead. Then I thought about all the other people in their lives who unintentionally do that every single day in the name of being supportive or preparing them for the world. I couldn't protect my daughters from the words of others, but I could praise their inner knowing and encourage them to listen intently. I could help my girls navigate their internal and external worlds so their life choices weren't blindly driven by all those external voices, like my life choices had been.

We all know so called good kids who did what their parents wanted. Hell, I just confessed to being one of them. Those kids joined the tennis team instead of the drama club only because the scholarship prospects were better. They became part of the science squad instead of the unofficial street hockey league that played every day until the street-lights came on. They worked a desk job with a 401(k) plan instead of starting a candle business. They went to law school, joined the military, or took over the family business.

On the road to "good," many kids stopped exploring their own version of a backyard swamp and made choices based on what someone else wanted for them. Not that there's anything wrong with a traditional career, but the trope of following someone else's path is a well-worn one. In fact, one study published in *Forbes* indicates that "a majority (65%) of respondents today work in the field their parents wanted for them."

And it's not just our parents' voices in our heads telling us what to do. Messages bombard us from all sides. We see them on billboards, we hear them on loudspeakers, we believe them in the depths of our hearts . . . and we feel powerless against them. Our minds are seduced and molded by what society tells us. We hear:

Stand out.
Fit in.
Don't rock the boat.
Go for the gold.
Walk the righteous path.
Do as I say.
Be strong.
Stop crying.
Don't question authority.
Think for yourself.
Be a man.

These messages can be confusing, especially when they conflict with how we feel inside. (Yes, I know we're only three chapters in, and I'm already harping on this point!) As social creatures who crave love and attention, we tend to take the path that will give us more of that, not less ... even if it means not doing what we really want. For a picture of what this looks like, let's jump in a time machine. It's the night before a big race, just when I'd started taking running more seriously.

It's 1:00 a.m. and I'm lying awake in my bed crying. For a fifteen-year-old, this is beyond embarrassing, the shame making me convulse even more. A cocktail of Pacific Northwest rain and sleet blasts the windows. Tears and sweat stain my sheets, and the ticking clock taunts my strained breath. The starting gun will go off at 9:00 a.m. sharp.

Today is the first race against my foremost rival—the best runner in our age group in British Columbia—and I am about to get zero sleep.

Determined to be well-rested for the race, I marched up to bed at 7:30 p.m. But going to bed before I was even tired proved to be the catalyst for this waking nightmare. Each hour I can't sleep breeds a growing anxiety. At 8:30 p.m. it didn't matter much, but by 10:30 p.m. I was falling apart. No breathing exercises helped calm my frayed nerves and racing heart.

My mother comes in, distraught by my inability to sleep, fretting over the stress a young boy is putting himself through.

She knows that I believe the measure of my goodness rests on the outcome of every single performance. Not that she *outwardly* puts this pressure on me. She isn't one of those parents who yells from the sidelines or gives stern lectures when I fall short. No, she knows this because there is something unsaid, something undone, something unfulfilled in her that makes her hope she can live through me. It's not intentional or malicious, but human, the pride of a loving parent. That *something* causes her own tears to fall, and I sense her heart breaking. She sees herself in me; she sees her own trauma in me; and now her deep scars are my newly formed wounds.

Over and over again she asks, "Do you not want to race?" And over and over I answer that I do. I want to show my strength and courage and make everyone proud. But what my heart wants at this time, during a seemingly normal teenage outburst of uncontrolled emotions, I do not understand until many years later.

What I needed was not for my mother to ask if I wanted to race but to tell me it was okay if I didn't. I needed my father to come upstairs and say, "Instead of racing tomorrow, let's play hooky. We can go hike a mountain and get a big breakfast." I needed them to let me know that I was good enough without that race. I needed to feel and experience love that was truly unconditional.

I didn't get what I needed, so I raced.

Afterwards, my coach looked at my gaunt face. I'd been flushed with adrenaline for fifteen agonizing minutes. My jaw was still clenched and my body stiff in anticipation of … something. Coach was old-school: stern yet caring. He said we needed to talk. He invited me over for tea after I warmed down and dried off.

He cut to the chase: "You look exhausted."

"Yes." I nodded. "That one took it out of me, for sure."

"You exhaust yourself obsessing and thinking about each race."

"Isn't visualization important?" I asked a bit sheepishly. He had, after all, recommended several books on the topic, which I'd gobbled up.

"Yes, to an extent," he said. "But you are not visualizing the race once or twice to get your bearings on how you'll feel, or imagining how it will go and how you'll respond to what might happen. You're exhausting yourself by running it over and over and over again in your mind. And you exhaust yourself by worrying about the outcome. Do you think that matters? Do you think you won't be a good runner if you don't win every race?"

"No," I lied.

"That boy you raced today, who beat you quite easily, he is beatable. With hard work, you have the ability to overtake him. But beating him doesn't make you better, because after him there will be someone else. What then? You are not good enough again? You need to run because you *want* to run. Because you like the competitive spirit of it. That's it."

Over the years I did my best to take his words to heart, but more often than not, I exhausted myself in worry, believing I wasn't good enough unless I won.

As we go through life, our collective actions take on meaning. We become a person who does "this" or does "that." We are viewed as *caring* or *responsible* or *flakey* because of what we do and have done. We accept the labels applied to us, which reinforces future behavior that keeps us consistently in those roles. Those actions form part of our identity: he's a champion runner; she's a mathlete; he's good at cooking; she's incredibly creative.

Our minds are jam-packed with these labels and corresponding concepts of how we are supposed to be in this world. If our actions don't match those labels, we risk rejection. The champion runner has to keep running. The mathlete must win competitions. The cook has to whip up gourmet food every time he's in the kitchen, and the creative is expected to up her game with each and every project.

No doubt that desire and ambition to perform is what drives us forward.; it is also clearly born of the human spirit. And no doubt we must also challenge ourselves in spite of our nerves and fear. Unchecked, however, they can metastasize into a never-ending need to excel. So, we double down on those labels to be accepted and maintain our place in the world. We accept this as our identity. As our success in our assigned roles is celebrated, we receive a nice little dopamine hit that encourages us along the same path of responding to external expectations—even if something feels off. This is how many of us end up on the hedonic treadmill: achieving that next level of "whatever," then returning to the same base level of happiness and needing to push even further the next time. Repeat.

But are we truly excelling and achieving if we're running someone else's race?

One night, while reading to my daughters, I came across a story called *The Lion Who Thought He Was a Sheep,* which resonated deeply. It goes like this:

There once was a lion who grew up in a flock of sheep, believing he was one of them. He would bleat like a sheep and eat grass like a sheep because that's what he learned to do. His lion tendencies were still there, however, and sometimes he would get angry or play rough with the flock. Over time he learned to behave himself, but he never felt like he fit with the others.

One day while the sheep were grazing, a huge jungle lion appeared. The sheep scattered, and the intruder was surprised to see one of his own among the flock. He walked up to this curious creature and said, "What are you doing here?"

"Don't eat me!" the lion begged.

The jungle lion shook his head and said, "You're not a sheep, and I'm not going to eat you. Come with me."

They walked together to a pond and the jungle lion urged him to look at his reflection.

It was the first time the lion had seen himself and he was shocked. He looked at the jungle lion, then again at his reflection and let out a mighty roar.

"I'm not a sheep, I am like you!"

"That's right," the jungle lion said. "Now stop acting like a sheep. You're a lion."

He roared again because he finally knew who he truly was.

When who we are inside doesn't match who the external world tells us we are, we try to reconcile the two. We use those external voices to compare ourselves to others, try to fit in, seek permission to be who we are, or accept the labels placed on us—just as the lion did. Fittingly, it was the mighty voice of another lion that helped the sheepish one see his true self.

Not all voices are the enemy, but when we equate "good" with the voice of acceptance and "bad" with the voice of rejection, we choose careers that don't light us up, friends who don't value us, and partners who don't respect us. We fall in line, follow the "shoulds," and ignore the feeling inside that tells us there's something more waiting for us when we present our authentic selves to the world. When standards are set by one loud group or individual, it limits our potential for embracing ourselves.

In Susan Cain's bestseller *Quiet: The Power of Introverts in a World That Can't Stop Talking*, she cites the bias shift towards extroversion that happened in the 1920s as more Americans became urbanites, capitalism boomed, and the self-help movement hit full swing. "At the onset of the Culture of Personality," Cain writes, "we were urged to develop an extroverted personality for frankly selfish reasons—as a way of outshining the crowd in a newly anonymous and competitive society. But nowadays we tend to think that becoming more extroverted not only makes us more successful, but also makes us better people. We see salesmanship as a way of sharing one's gifts with the world."

Prestigious educational institutions like Harvard and Yale began to give precedence to the confident intelligence of extroverts over the quiet genius of introverts, both in admissions and in campus culture. The value society placed on extroversion trickled down to grade school classrooms as well. Children were moved from single desks to group tables in the effort to educate them in a more social, cooperative way. But what about the child who doesn't learn well in groups? Albert Einstein, Elon Musk, Steve Wozniak, and J. K. Rowling are all self-professed introverts.

This isn't meant to diminish the contributions of extroverts, as that group has its fair share of change-makers, but how can we say one group is better than the other? What our society values shifts over time, so if you're an introvert growing up in a culture that favors extroverts, you may contort yourself in order to feel valued by society.

To fit in, you may bleat like a sheep, even if you're a lion.

4

Belonging

I long, as does every human being, to be at home wherever I find myself.

~ Maya Angelou

External messages about good and bad (and how we interpret them) impact how we see the world, how we see ourselves, how we behave and, ultimately, our felt sense of belonging, which is a core human need. When external and internal messages clash, that inner turmoil can make us want to hide our true selves—which isn't exactly a winning strategy when trying to fit in on this cliquey place we call earth.

According to Abraham Maslow's Hierarchy of Needs theory, our actions are motivated by certain physiological and psychological needs that fall into a certain order in terms of fulfilment. Basic needs are at the bottom of the hierarchy and must be fulfilled before more advanced ones are. The hierarchy looks like this:

1. Physiological needs: Food, water, sleep, sex, breathing, homeostasis

2. Safety and security needs: Financial security, health and wellness, safety against accidents and injury

3. Social needs: Friendships, romantic relationships, family relationships, social groups, community groups

4. Esteem needs: Appreciation, respect, accomplishment, recognition

5. Self-actualization needs: Self-awareness, personal growth, living up to one's potential

This certainly makes sense—if you don't have enough food to eat, you're probably not dwelling on your complicated relationship with your mother. And if you're living paycheck to paycheck, you may be less concerned with accolades and a trophy collection than with paying rent.

If those basic needs are met, however, our brain turns its ever-vigilant attention to solving (i.e. worrying about) the next item on Maslow's list: social needs.

Let's imagine someone who was excluded from playground games as a kid, cut from teams, and ignored by a parent (intentionally or unintentionally). Later in life this person suffers the crushing pain of heartbreak, constantly falls short in the eye of their boss, and struggles to maintain friendships.

With regards to success, this person may be more driven by social needs than esteem needs. Perhaps they people-please to gain approval or follow the status quo to gain acceptance. Instead of following their own path, they lean into anything that provides a sense of belonging, and all because their social bucket still needs filling.

Belonging is central to our social needs. It makes us feel safe and secure and provides the shelter from life's emotional storms. The comfort in belonging to a family, a friend group, or a community gives meaning to our existence and actually brings us back to ourselves. It is in this need for belonging that, ironically, we allow ourselves to find solace in our individuality. Kind of like the rebellious teenager who locks himself in his room, cranks up the tunes, and pours his heart out into his journal to try to figure out who he is.

This exploration of who we are and where we belong as we transition from child to adult is held in the balance of how secure we feel in our home life. In other words, it is precisely *because* he knows Mom and Dad (or gran and gramps) will be there for him that he is able to explore his identity without fear of being cast out of the nest. Cue the music: "Parents just don't understand!"

Without a strong sense of belonging, the ground beneath us feels unsteady, like it could give way at any moment. One bad move and the group might cast us out because we're not like them. Our propensity towards belonging to a tribe is innate; we are social creatures who take refuge in the security of the group. We used to sit around campfires with fellow hunters and foragers. Now it's ball clubs and political parties. Even belonging to a book club or gym can offer a secure feeling of kinship.

Or one of the OG clubs: church!

Jehovah's Witnesses come by my house each week offering a ticket to salvation. They ask me to join the other 144,000 faithful Christians who will be resurrected as immortal spiritual beings to spend eternity with God. I can tell by the Santa Claus twinkle in the gentleman's eye, as he holds his wife's hand, that he feels a deep sense of belonging amongst the JW's. But like the first time I spiked my hair with Dippity Do, wore a fake diamond earing and a puka shell necklace . . . sometimes you just know when something isn't for you. Each time I hear their pitch, I'm transported back to church, fidgeting in my tight, itchy clothes. My mom dressed me in pants and a button-down shirt so I would fit in with the rest of the congregation—as many parents do—but I never felt like I belonged there.

Fitting in and belonging are two separate things. Actually, they're polar opposites.

Fitting in asks us to appraise a situation and decide how we need to act to gain acceptance of the group (in my case, puka shells). Belonging requires us to simply be who we are because who we are is acceptable. When you conform to gain acceptance, the clothes feel uncomfortable; but when you're blissfully splashing around with other swamp-dwellers, you feel exactly where you belong.

So, why do we try to fit in when it just feels … off? Assuming the basic needs of security, food, and shelter are otherwise met, the giant, looming threat to true belonging, the thing that causes us to hide our weaknesses, insecurities, and indiscretions, forcing our shadow into the corner is … shame.

Author and researcher Brené Brown defines shame as "the intensely painful feeling or experience of believing that we are flawed and therefore unworthy of love and belonging—something we've experienced, done, or failed to do makes us unworthy of connection."

Because belonging is so critical to our social, safety, and even physiological needs, shame is literally an existential threat. We are no longer vulnerable to saber-toothed tiger attacks while wandering the savannah alone, but the primitive part of our brain thinks we are. We hide anything that could separate us from the protection of our group, yet we've simultaneously created a society where our every move is scrutinized.

Watching people cast stones of judgement at others has become somewhat of a sport in our culture. We see it unfold in posts, comments, and tweets; say something unpopular or unacceptable and you risk being shunned. We see it play out in cancel culture, where someone is publicly shamed for their so-called transgressions. This is a form of ostracism that can take place online or in person. In this culture, you can be defined by, and punished for, your worst moment. Or simply for being you.

Another one of shame's more Machiavellian outcomes is self-censorship. Downstream from that, free speech drowns.

But who decides what's acceptable and not acceptable? What's good and what's bad? Are they not the same people who are running from their own shame and turning it into a weapon against others? Have they disowned their shadow selves to the point that they can't tolerate it in others?

From social movements to political affiliations to the team Edward versus team Jacob competitions that came out of the Twilight book series by Stephanie Meyer (yes, my daughters have demanded my allegiance to Edward), and a laundry list of other polarizing topics, a person's position signals which tribe they belong to. This "with us or against us" polarization has divided society along ideological lines with the antipathy rising to a fever pitch. And the division is all rooted in this sense of belonging.

Whether or not you agree with the reasons for someone's "cancellation," it's not a stretch to assume the threat of ostracization forces individuals to shove their skeletons even deeper into the closet. Why share something shameful if it could result in being shunned? Our shadow selves sing and dance to the soundtrack of shame, and there never seems to be a shortage of music.

For many of us, shame ran amok during our high school and/or college years when belonging felt like life or death (and to our primitive brain, it was). For instance, if everyone did something you hadn't done, the fear of being outed and then ostracized was very real. Coming-of-age movies like *American Pie*, *Mean Girls*, *The Breakfast Club*, and dozens more center around this universal need to belong and the intense peer pressure to fit in. These resonate because we've all felt it, but the joke's on us because fitting in is never the path to true belonging.

When I was in high school, I decided to wait for "the one" to have sex with because I wanted to be old enough to make what I considered to be a very important decision. By the time I graduated and was off to college, however, I decided it was time. Whether that was my raging hormones or the fact that most of my friends were reportedly already doing the deed and I felt pressured to fit in, I don't know.

So, as if starring in my own coming-of-age film, my college girlfriend and I decided to drive to a special spot where we could be intimate, as much as a couple could be in the backseat of a Buick. Yep, an actual Buick. How's that for classy and cliché?

Naturally, I was nervous. Everything I knew about sex came from school learning, which posited recreational sex as bad, while providing no actual tips on how to be a good lover, which forced one to seek counsel from friends, who simply raved about how awesome it was without sharing any details as to exactly why or how. This was before the days of the top-quality sex ed you could get on Porn Hub (note the sarcasm). To say I didn't have a clear picture of what to do or what to expect is a magnum sized understatement, especially when it came to the emotional aspect of love making that *no one* was talking about.

I wanted to be caring and attentive, but mostly I just knew it was important to be good at it. No pressure, right? She was also a virgin, so neither of us knew what we were doing. It ended up being awkward, unenjoyable, and traditionally incomplete, with no climax for either of us (the tantric arts were not yet on my radar). Afterwards, she asked a question no man ever wants to hear: "Is it supposed to feel like that?"

Excuse me, what? Based on what I'd gleaned from my friends' ramblings on the transformative magic of doing the deed, her reaction was not in my sexual lexicon. What about: "Don't stop!" or "Harder!" Goodness gracious.

Unsurprisingly, my libido shut down for the night; Richard and the twins went off duty. Then, just as I was begging them to stand at attention once again, my girlfriend teared up and asked, "Is it me?" Fuck. The Buick felt more like a prison than a love shack, and I most certainly didn't want to talk about it.

Turns out, life doesn't always mimic art, so I didn't get to live out that triumphant scene in *American Pie* where Finch and Stifler's mom achieve backseat glory. Quite the opposite. For an insecure nineteen-year-old man who had just broken his moral code and decided not to wait, that was not the positive or encouraging experience I needed.

To combat the voice in my head that pointed out once again how I wasn't good enough, I tried to chalk it up to inexperience and human nature. But, over time, I felt worse and worse. My feelings of inadequacy led to a fear of having sex again—with her or anyone else. Unsurprisingly, we broke up. Whenever someone asked what happened, I didn't want to talk about it, and for a very long time.

Brené Brown explains my behavior more eloquently: "Shame hates it when we reach out and tell our story. It hates having words wrapped around it—it can't survive being shared. Shame loves secrecy. When we bury our story, the shame metastasizes."

That first sexual experience metastasized into a shame soup that simmered in the substratum of my shadow for years on end. It fed the wrong wolf.

The emotional trauma that resulted from this single experience completely changed how I felt physically. Tightness filled my body, my back ached, and my jaw seemed perpetually clenched.

Bessel van der Kolk says in his seminal work, *The Body Keeps Score*, "Traumatized people chronically feel unsafe inside their bodies: The past is alive in the form of gnawing interior discomfort. As long as you keep secrets and suppress information, you are fundamentally at war with yourself . . . The critical issue is allowing yourself to know what you know. That takes an enormous amount of courage."

Fast-forward several years to couples counseling with my wife. We were young and both struggling in our marriage, believing we had different wants and needs that couldn't be reconciled. Neither of us wanted a divorce (thankfully), but our grievances were showing up in the bedroom and spilling over into the rest of our personal and professional lives.

One of the many exercises we were tasked with was called the "mirror exercise." Like a mirror, we had to reflect the other person's thoughts and feelings back to them. Repeating what your partner shares helps them feel heard, seen, and understood. Taking this a step further, we also shared what we saw in each other—honoring both the pain and the goodness.

We discovered that our differences were mostly the projections of our own fear and pain. This was a powerful lesson. As it were, we'd both had a negative first sexual experience. Learning this about my wife was both comforting and painful—painful because she, too, had buried her shame and carried its heavy boulders in her heart. It was comforting because sharing our stories softened the sharp edges of our individual perspectives of "badness."

With this newfound sense of vulnerability and trust, we shared our other traumatic experiences. The stones of judgement my wife and I had been collecting were weighing us down. By learning to see each other and, by reflection, ourselves as whole humans who contained both lightness and darkness, judgement gave way to understanding, compassion, and acceptance. We embraced our shadows and replaced guilt and shame with gratitude for the lessons our experiences had given us. The great Farsi poet Rumi, of course, puts a much more poetic spin on it: "The dark thought, the shame, the malice, meet them at the door laughing, and invite them in. Be grateful for whoever comes, because each has been sent as a guide from beyond."

Living from our shadows, we could not see each other's beauty and light.

Instead of using pain as a weapon to wage war on each other, we learned to see each other's wounds as "the place where light enters the soul," to borrow again from Rumi. In other words, we shifted from judgement, shame, and fear to acceptance, healing, and trust. It strengthened our shared experience as a couple, bringing us closer to each other and creating a deep sense of belonging.

But belonging isn't just something we crave in intimate relationships. "Being able to feel safe with other people is probably the single most important aspect of mental health," van der Kolk writes. "Safe connections are fundamental to meaningful and satisfying lives." Our shameful shadow can put a room divider between us and those safe connections. Without my wife and me sharing our stories and coming to a place of acceptance (for ourselves and each other), our marriage—if we did make it—would have been awfully dark and lonely.

Beyond belonging, there is a lot going on inside our crafty little brains to keep us safe, and becoming aware of it can inform our decisions. We think we need to do things a certain way, until we realize we're unconsciously creating our own obstacles and limitations.

For this, we dive from the tip of the iceberg to swim in the cold, dark waters below.

5

Unconscious

The person is free who lives as they wish, neither compelled, nor hindered, nor limited—whose choices aren't hampered, whose desires succeed, and who don't fall into what repels them. Who wishes to live in deception— tripped up, mistaken, undisciplined, complaining, in a rut? No one. These are base people who don't live as they wish; and so, no base person is free.

~ Epictetus, Discourses

How much can be communicated without saying a word? Max Major attempts to answer this question with his mentalism act on *America's Got Talent*. With his leather jacket and slicked-back hair, Max stands calmly, coolly, and confidently in front of the judges.

A prerecorded video of him behind the bar of an Irish pub starts playing on the screen behind him. In the video, Max describes his background as a bartender and how it prepared him to become a mentalist. Spending countless hours observing people, he learned a lot about human nature and the power of perception. Max performs a few tricks to demonstrate, then leaves the bar to walk down an empty, café-lined street while talking to the camera. He asserts, "Our thoughts are a combination of our own ideas and the choices that other people want us to make."

That's a slightly menacing statement, but the happy music and Max's charisma keep things light. When the video ends, Max says he's going to show us something impossible, then reveal how he did it. For magicians, this is the ultimate sin. But Max isn't a traditional magician or even a psychic; he's a mentalist.

Mentalists draw from intuition and psychology to perform incredible "mind reading" feats. By tuning in to body language and harnessing the power of suggestion, they can expand reality and produce psychological experiences for the audience.

Standing onstage, Max asks the audience members to close their eyes, focus on the image they see in their mind's eye, then draw what they just saw. He then turns to Howie Mandel, one of the three judges, and asks him to close his eyes, imagine a billboard, then draw the image he sees on the billboard.

Max pulls his own drawing from a sealed envelope and reveals a sun with a happy face in the middle. When Max asks Howie to show what he has drawn, shockingly it's the exact same image! Then the entire audience holds up their papers. Yep, they all drew that very same smiling sun.

How did Max get everyone to sketch exactly what he wanted them to? The video he played at the beginning of his act was full of sunny images and messages hidden in plain sight. There was a sunny drink coaster, a *Welcome to Sunny California* sign, a chalkboard drawing of a sun, and more. He was planting subliminal seeds without Howie and the audience even knowing it.

What Max is demonstrating is the power of the unconscious mind and the massive role it plays in our thoughts. The distinction between *conscious* and *unconscious* was popularized by Austrian neurologist Sigmund Freud in 1915. If you're struggling to remember those high school lessons on Freud, here's a refresher:

Part of Freud's theory suggests that the human mind is divided into two parts: a conscious part and an unconscious part. Both impact our behavior. The conscious mind encompasses everything we are aware of; the unconscious includes memories, feelings, dreams, urges. Our unconscious mind influences our actions often without us knowing.

Let's pause a minute to address unconscious versus subconscious. Freud initially used the terms interchangeably but landed on *unconscious* to avoid confusion, so that's usually what you'll see in academic papers. *Subconscious* is sometimes used either to mean the same as *unconscious* or to suggest a sort of middle layer of the mind, where information that lies just below consciousness can be accessed through introspection or self-reflection.

For the sake of simplicity (and to avoid a debate on the topic), let's use *unconscious* to mean anything below the level of conscious awareness. Think of a computer hard drive. The unconscious mind, like the hard drive, holds all the information for everything you have ever experienced. Freud used the image of an iceberg with the tip above the water's surface representing the conscious mind, and the giant mountain of ice underwater representing the unconscious.

On an average day, perhaps you wake up, smell the roses, eat some breakfast, catch the subway to work, see a billboard for a nice leather bag, marvel at your boss' new car, chat with coworkers about the latest Netflix series (which included product placement for some actor's new brand of gin), wince at your partner's facial expression when you arrive home late from work, scroll through social media and pause on a sponsored post for how to live your dream life, turn on TV to see a happy family arriving at their VRBO rental . . . and on and on.

Every second of every day, your mind is processing and storing data. It also maintains your body temperature at a balmy 98.6 degrees Fahrenheit, regulates your breathing, eliminates toxins, and generally keeps everything humming along in a harmonious state of homeostasis. So pause for a moment and thank your amazing body for, you know, taking care of you without you having to do much! Then ask yourself, how much of this are you aware of?

Although the actual amount is unknown, neurologists and scientific assessments suggest that unconscious activity is in control of, or at least influences, our thoughts and behavior up to 95 percent of the time. That means most of our emotions, decisions, and actions are motivated from below the level of conscious awareness. Yep, much like commercial flights, the majority of our waking hours are spent on autopilot.

This isn't all bad. Autopilot is extremely helpful for routine tasks such as brushing your teeth, making an omelet, driving a car, and other recurring tasks that don't require you to think about how to do it each time. Like when you space out while driving home, yet still manage to make all the correct turns to get there. But when you make decisions based on unconscious information, information that may have been seeded in your mind by an external source—perhaps something you read or saw or heard—your behavior may change without you realizing it.

Enter Eddie Bernays, a pioneer in modern advertising and public relations, who happened to be Sigmund Freud's nephew. In the early 1900s, Freud's theories successfully jumped from the classroom to the boardroom of booming capitalist America.

Bernays, hired by the American Tobacco Company, knew how to tap into the unconscious of his target audiences. His ads encouraged women to start smoking, a habit that was almost exclusively male back then. Bernays's cigarette ads featured sophisticated women with lines like, *I smoke a Lucky instead of eating sweets* and *Believe in yourself!* Bernays also provided propaganda for the 1954 Guatemalan coup d'état that led to the overthrow of President

Jacobo Arbenz Guzman. These examples outline just how pernicious external influence over a person's volition can be when used for less-than-savory purposes—something we need to wake up to as a society.

The unconscious mind collects the information, ideas, and images it is repeatedly exposed to, and then executes with precision: you buy cigarettes, you draw a sun, or you even overthrow a government.

In 1927, Lehman Brothers executive Paul Mazur suggested the following in an article in the *Harvard Business Review*: "We must shift America from a needs to a desires culture. People must be trained to desire, to want new things even before the old had been entirely consumed. We must shape a new mentality in America. Man's desires must overshadow his needs."

Which, I guess, falls somewhere between Maslow's esteem and self-actualization needs.

Some eighty plus years later, *Thinking Fast and Slow* author Daniel Kahneman offers this take: "A reliable way to make people believe in falsehoods is frequent repetition because familiarity is not easily distinguished from truth. Authoritarian institutions and marketers have always known this fact."

Psyops, anyone?

The unconscious mind plays a huge role in what we believe and how we behave. And, yeah, it can be manipulated. Simply knowing this can help us become more discerning consumers of information. You should understand that unconscious messages don't always come in the form of ads, propaganda, and other conspicuous formats. Most messages are much more subtle.

Let's say you suddenly decided to become a runner. And not just someone who runs the annual Thanksgiving Turkey Trot; you want to run a marathon.

And not just any 26.2-mile race; you want to run the Boston Marathon. You believe this to be an independent choice that you've just discovered hidden inside you.

The postulation that your wants are entirely your own is what the French social scientist and polymath René Girard calls "the romantic lie." At its foundation is mimetic theory. *Mimetic* derives from the ancient Greek word *mimesis*, meaning "imitation" or "mimicry." The theory proposes that we imitate what other people want.

In his book *Wanting: The Power of Mimetic Desire in Everyday Life*, author Luke Burgis builds off mimetic theory by explaining that, "According to Girard, humans don't desire anything independently. This affects the way we choose partners, friends, careers, clothes, and vacation destinations. Mimetic desire is responsible for the formation of our very identities. It explains the enduring relevancy of Shakespeare's plays, why Peter Thiel decided to be the first investor in Facebook, and why our world is growing more divided as it becomes more connected."

So, no, according to mimetic theory, your Boston Marathon idea didn't originate with you. It was likely the result of your environment: a conversation among a running group that you overheard at the coffee shop, friends talking about "crushing Boston," a magazine ad for running shoes with someone triumphantly crossing the finish line, and so forth.

Ultimately, mimetic theory posits that mimetic desire—wanting what other people want—leads to conflict and rivalry as individuals compete for the same thing. Once this common want spreads among a community and rival coalitions threaten the community's peace, scapegoating occurs. Groups identify a single person as responsible and assign blame for the conflict, which leads to punishment of that person and/or expulsion from the community.

Sounds a little like what's happening in cancel culture, doesn't it? But wait, there's more.

According to the Colloquium on Violence & Religion, an international association of scholars and practitioners who are dedicated to developing, critiquing, and applying mimetic theory to violence and religion: "Scapegoating also operates in individuals at the level of identity. We all construct identities over someone or something else. I'm a woman, not a man. I'm a liberal not a conservative. I'm an atheist not a believer. And most problematically, I'm good not bad. When we need some other person or group to be bad so we can maintain our sense of ourselves as good by comparison, we have engaged in scapegoating. We are using others to solidify our identity the same way a community uses a scapegoat to solve its internal conflict."

By making someone else the villain, we get to be the hero. By ostracizing someone, we strengthen our position inside the group. Once again, we're giving in to polarized thinking. This is belonging gamesmanship, if you will. It's intentional, yet often unconsciously woven into our human makeup and influenced by what we read, hear, and watch; it is the sunny pictures we encounter everywhere.

Sometimes our unconscious may lead us astray, but it was evolutionarily designed to protect us. In addition to the external messages we receive and the epic origin tales we tell ourselves, how we judge something as good or bad is partly Darwinian.

Negativity bias is a psychological phenomenon that allows negative events to have more impact on us than positive ones. It causes us to dwell on the negative more than the positive. According to neurological studies, negative stimuli trigger a larger brain response than positive stimuli. This is one reason traumas (even traumas with a little *t*) are so hard to overcome yet so important to heal. Negativity is hardwired into us.

Early humans relied on negativity bias for survival. It allowed their default mode of thinking, their unconscious, to be constantly on alert for what could eat them or harm them. Assuming the rustling in the bush is a saber-toothed tiger versus a bunny had survival value. Dwelling on the negative is one way the brain tries to keep us safe.

"The brain is like Velcro for negative experiences and Teflon for positive ones," says psychologist Rick Hanson, author of *Hardwiring Happiness*. This partly explains why we expect negative outcomes instead of positive ones:

I'm going to fail the test.
I'll forget my lines and freeze onstage.
I won't finish the race.
He/she won't ask me out on another date.
I'll lose everything.

Then we slide down the slippery slope of unconsciously turning those outcomes into character traits:

I'm stupid.
I have no talent.
I'm undeserving.
I'm unlovable.
I'm a failure.

When our interpretation of positive and negative, good and bad turns inward, it can feed our shadow selves. The same stories that guide our moral actions can also serve as means by which we judge ourselves. But the good news is we are not powerless over these stories. By understanding our unconscious mind, we can consciously make different choices.

Victor Frankl, psychiatrist, concentration-camp survivor, and author of *Man's*

Search for Meaning, said, "Between stimulus and response there is a space. In that space is our power to choose our response. In our response lies our growth and our freedom."

We can choose how we interpret the messages we receive. We can acknowledge negativity bias while consciously choosing to look on the bright side, as they say. We can honor our feelings while challenging our thoughts. Both are possible. This is maturity.

Whether it's from religious teachings, parental flub-ups, Times Square billboards, or high school traumas, how we perceive good and bad is shaped by *something* (or, more accurately, many *somethings*). Some influences we consciously let in, but most are unknowingly downloaded into our unconscious.

Regardless of where the influence comes from, we are responsible for the choices we make. And it's possible to bring awareness to the unconscious. According to Dr. Leon F. Seltzer, author of *Paradoxical Strategies in Psychotherapy*: "There's no way that you can reach your full potential until you gain entry into much of what exists below your awareness—that is, make both the unconscious and subconscious conscious—and, at last, come to positive terms with what, unknowingly, has been sabotaging you."

Seltzer is pointing to shadow integration. As defined by Carl Jung, this is the "process of bringing the hidden parts of the Self into consciousness."

Shadow integration reminds us that we have more power over ourselves than we think. By understanding the psychological forces at play, we can challenge our thinking and dig a little deeper. Where did those messages come from, and from whom? Did they enter consciously (with our permission) or unconsciously (without us knowing)? Do they resonate with our internal voice or create conflict? Are they positive or negative affirmations? And do they lead us where we want to go, or do they hold us back?

This is just part of the puzzle. Identifying a bunch of disparate messages and where they come from can be confusing. What does it all add up to? What does it mean? As I've mentioned in this book, we rely on stories to make sense of the world. We can do the same to make sense of ourselves.

6

Perception

There is no good or bad without us, there is only perception. There is the event itself and the story we tell ourselves about what it means.

~ Ryan Holiday, "The Obstacle is the Way"

It was while attending college in North Carolina on an athletic scholarship that I tore my Achilles. Determined to heal as fast as possible so I could run again, I practically lived on the stationary bike or with a bag of frozen corn pressed to my heel, only leaving for trips to the physiotherapist.

Surely, the injury would heal, but progress was slow and torturous. Eventually, my therapy graduated to interval training where I would walk for forty-five seconds, run for fifteen seconds, walk for forty-five … all for an agonizing thirty minutes in a grassy field. Every two days, the running interval increased by fifteen seconds. It was utter hell, and I couldn't understand what I had done to deserve it.

Rehab dragged on like a Pacific Northwest winter—all rain and darkness with no promise of sunshine. I yo-yoed between hope and despair, stressing over whether my tendon fibers would ever coalesce. Had my mother dipped me in the River Styx when I was a baby? As the Greek myth goes, Achilles' mother plunged his infant body into the protective waters of the river, holding him by one foot so all but his heel was submerged and made safe from harm. But it was an arrow that pierced that single point of weakness and ended his life. My life revolved around running, so this single injury felt like it was threatening my very mortality. Achilles, I feel ya.

Tossing and turning in my bunk late into the night became a regular occurrence and led to increased homesickness. Who said North Carolina was one of the most beautiful states? I wanted to have a word with them.

It wasn't until I committed the ultimate sin of an injured athlete that I finally broke: I went online to check race results. This is the runner's equivalent of scrolling through your ex-lover's Instagram account. Nothing good can ever come of it, and you know that, but you do it anyway.

This self-destructive search was how I found out that I had been removed from Canada's world cross-country team because of my health status and inability to compete. That bit of news was the proverbial match to the powder keg of my negativity that allowed it to explode all over the place. But I was determined that I would be more Shakespearean than a character in Greek mythology. Yes, I—not the mythological gods of various running bureaucracies—would write my own dramatic ending to this story.

So, I impulsively dropped out of school, forfeiting my athletic scholarship.

I told the university that my coach back home in Vancouver was sick, so I needed to be with him. Yes, he'd had a near-death episode, but that's not why I left—and my university coach knew it.

My athletic scholarship had been one of the largest awarded in my district that year, so it was announced in front of thousands at the school's year-end ceremony and written up in the local paper. When I'd accepted the scholarship, I had declared it a stepping stone to the Olympics—and now I was trashing all of it. This, however, was no romantic or poetic ending. The pride of my friends and family disappeared in an instant. The shame of that event was beyond anything I had ever experienced.

If I had actually died of a broken heart, as I had thought I might, my epitaph surely would have read *overreacted.*

Upon returning home, I went to community college. People surely wondered (as did I) what was wrong with me. Could I not hack it at a big-name school? Was I not good enough? What happened to all that big talk about the Olympics? In an unconsciously arrogant way, I believed a spotlight was shining on me, and everyone was wondering what I was doing instead of focusing on their own lives.

"When we fail, we think all eyes are on us," self-help author Neil Pasricha writes. "We think it's all about us! Sucking at a job means being publicly humiliated and sleeping with a tray of club sandwiches or living in a box on the street. A bad breakup means no more relationships ever. One rejected college application means you're clearly an airhead whose life is about to get stuck in a world of grueling, minimum-wage pain. We take tiny strings of trouble and extrapolate them into huge problems with our entire identities always on the line."

Shortly after I left North Carolina, my former coach was let go because of sexual harassment charges (rightly or wrongly, I don't know), and so I told everyone that's why I'd left. I used him as my scapegoat.

Truth be told, I didn't know why I'd pulled up stakes and left. Something just came over me—a deep feeling of "something's not right." I didn't question it or analyze it or even realize what was happening because I acted before my conscious brain could catch up. I told myself a story about being injury prone and never being able to compete at that high of a level again because of my injury, so there was no point in being there. Then I was left scrambling for a plausible reason to tell other people. And so, I lied.

In an attempt to make sense of the world, we turn events into stories that we tell ourselves and other people—we interpret our experiences and write a narrative from our individual viewpoint. Then we assign meaning to the narrative and accept that as the truth.

Of all the didactic Zen Buddhist parables, possibly the most well-known one comes to mind here:

> A farmer has a horse for many years; it helps him earn his livelihood and raise his son. One day, the horse runs away. His neighbor says sympathetically, "Such bad luck."
>
> The farmer replies, "Maybe. Who knows?"
>
> The next day, the horse makes its way back home, bringing with it another horse. The neighbor says with a smile, "Such good luck."
>
> The farmer replies, "Maybe. Who knows?"
>
> The following day, the farmer's son rides the new horse and seeks to tame it. In the process, he breaks his leg. The neighbor says sympathetically, "Such bad luck."
>
> The farmer replies, "Maybe. Who knows?"
>
> Then, the military comes to the village to draft all able-bodied young men to fight in a war. The son is exempt from the draft because of his broken leg.

You can guess what the neighbor said, and how the farmer replied. Good luck and bad luck are the meaning the neighbor assigns to the events. He uses these stories to make sense of what's happening, whereas the farmer assigns no meaning to the events and deals with what is. In my case, I saw my running career and my identity as a runner slipping away while I was recovering from injury. But were they really? Who knows. I never let it play out. Even though plenty of athletes are injured yet still return to their sport, I believed my own story that my running career was over.

Instead of choosing the harder "I might be wrong, so I'll keep working at it" path that is always accompanied by a valuable lesson, I chose to shrivel up into a ball of self-righteousness. "I'll break up with them before they break up with me!" Later in life, I learned that growth stems from being wrong, not from being right. A willingness to challenge your own stories and beliefs is incredibly valuable . . . but incredibly difficult.

It's difficult because we attach meaning to our stories. We label the thing that happened to us or is happening around us in the world as good or bad.

So, are good and bad just mental constructs that help us make sense of life? We decide what's painful or joyous, happy or sad, disappointing or surprising, meaningless or meaningful? And is their meaning completely subjective?

If a car reliably gets you from point A to point B and doesn't cost much to operate or maintain, is it a good car? What if that same car blows a tire, spins out of control on the highway, and smashes into the center divider? Would it still be a good car?

Let's use a more extreme example. Is killing someone bad? What if that someone is Hitler or Osama bin Laden?

This gets into the *very* grey area of morality, which is why good and bad are such sticky wickets. Can something be bad in one context, but good or at least accepted in another? In what situations does the end justify the means? That's not an easy line to draw.

To function in society and coexist with other humans, our wayward minds need some consensus of what is good and what is bad. Rules, laws, and social norms provide such guardrails. But if each society determines where to set those guardrails based on its own set of moral codes and values, could it be said that no moral truths hold for all people at all times?

Play that out and our own moral code has no special status; it is but one among many. So, who's right if different groups can't agree on what's good and bad?

Moral absolutism suggests that actions are intrinsically right or wrong, good or bad, regardless of the situation. Meaning stealing is always bad (even if you're starving) and killing is never justified (even in war).

But if good and bad could be distinguished by a simple line in the sand, our prisons would be full of soldiers who'd been called to arms by their nations. Let's revisit Maslow. As you'll recall, physiological needs (food, water, shelter) and safety needs rank as more imperative than social needs (relationships and community). If you were to construct a morality based on the Hierarchy of Needs, then punishment for stealing would be better to suffer than dying of starvation. So, we can understand the motivation to steal a loaf of bread—and write one of the great novels about it (that's Les Misérables in you're scratching your head). But moral absolutism disregards the nuance of human psychology.

Moral relativism, by contrast, acknowledges that people disagree about morality, so there is no universal standard that applies to everyone. Right and wrong/good and bad aren't fixed. They depend on the context and can evolve over time.

Digging further, meta-ethical moral relativism suggests morality can only be judged within its cultural context, relative to other cultures—meaning there is no objective truth. Wearing shorts in the United States is widely accepted. Not so much in Egypt, India, or many other countries where it would be considered inappropriate and/or disrespectful. So, is wearing shorts bad? It depends on where you are.

Normative relativism is the view that moral judgment can only happen within the context of that culture's societal norms. That means an outsider can't judge the actions of a culture as good or bad, right or wrong. To use our fashion example again, this means an Egyptian visiting the United States can't condemn the wearing of shorts, even if it's culturally inappropriate in their home country. Although I'm not sure if exceptions can be made for fashion faux pas?

Okay, let's complicate things even more.

According to a research study, people in different societal and cultural groups may endorse the same values but connect different behaviors with them. For example, we might all agree that protecting the environment is a value we hold, but practicing water conservation may be more associated with that value in places where water is scarce as opposed to places where it's abundant.

The value of equality may be enacted as equal pay initiatives in countries where gender equality is promoted, but as some other policy in countries that are less focused on equalizing the status of men and women. People in different cultures may agree that a certain value, like equality, is important, but differ on what behaviors support that value.

We may rationalize that our own values are based in logic, but we'd have to acknowledge that much of that logic is rooted in culture and family. We view our values as superior to others' because we rationalize them and can't see our blind spots. We can logic ourselves into believing we're right ... because being wrong is bad.

Take the chasm between the Democrats and Republicans in the United States, which some say has progressed to an all-out culture war following the election of Donald Trump. Both sides claim to be right while blaming and invalidating the other for issues ranging from unemployment and immigration to climate change, health care, and national security.

Culture wars, as we mentioned earlier, are defined as "disagreements about cultural and social beliefs between groups, especially between people with more conservative opinions and people with more progressive opinions." When these opinions are rooted in morality, they're even more polarizing. For instance, Right-wing conservatives lean on "traditional values" to combat liberal agendas, particularly those that support abortion, race equality, and LGBTQ rights. And in-turn, Left-wing liberals do the same in reverse. With no universal moral authority, is it surprising we're constantly on a treadmill of perpetual division?

The irony is that most people's hearts are in the right place. They want a moral code separating right from wrong, good from bad. The problem is not everyone agrees on where that line should be drawn because we all see the world through our own lens. Where we're born, which socioeconomic class we belong to, what culture and/or religion we follow, what opportunities are available (or not)—these all impact how we see the world.

Let's imagine two people are gazing at the same hill. One person is young and fit; the other is out of shape and wearing a heavy backpack. If you ask both people how steep the hill is, will their answers be the same?

According to researcher and psychologist Dennis Proffit, the answer is, no.

Our physical ability affects our perception, so the fit person will actually see a lower-grade hill than his less-capable climbing partner. Likewise, someone who is tired will view a set distance as longer than someone who is energized. And a football kicker who misses several field goals in a row will see the goal posts as narrower than a kicker with a more successful record.

Perception is not reality, yet it is *our* reality. And how we perceive is the product of our experiences. Past climbs, walks, and kicks impact how we judge the one in front of us. Past failures, setbacks, and traumas affect our perceived ability to succeed. In this way we can convince ourselves that the hill in front of us is too steep to climb when a simple change in the story we tell ourselves could turn Mount Everest into a walk in the park.

Writer Anaïs Nin said, "We don't see things as they are, we see things as *we* are."

This reminds me of being stuck on the side of the road one hot summer day, three hundred miles from home, with half a Clif bar, only a few swigs of water, and a cell phone with 25 percent battery life and one bar of reception.

Some four hours earlier, I had pulled my motorbike over to take in the view of the canyon from the Trans-Canada Highway—before me was a canvas painted with the grandeur only nature can create. I was so excited to see the view, write in my journal, and smoke a cigar that I left the key in the ignition. My bike's battery died, leaving me stranded. It was August, so I sat on the burning asphalt in the sliver of shade cast by my motorbike while I contemplated my next move.

I could lament my bad luck, letting anger and frustration boil over, but that wouldn't get me out of my predicament. Further, it would ruin the lovely trip I was enjoying up until this point and dim the stunning views around me. I remembered advice from a friend: "Reframing allows us to embrace life as it happens to us and to paint the circumstances that come to us from a palette of our own choosing."

I managed to fire off a couple quick texts: one to my wife with my geolocation so she could send a tow truck, and another to a friend who lived in a small town about an hour away, asking him to be on standby in case the tow truck was a no-show. All that was left to do was breathe slowly, trust things would work out, patiently wait, and enjoy the view.

The tow truck did eventually arrive and give me a jump, but I was so tired and parched that instead of riding my bike all the way home in the middle of the night, I motored to my friend's house. This situation offered up a beautiful opportunity to catch up with a friend—because of how I chose to see it. This is a choice we all have.

Side note: I later learned from three separate sources that you can jump a motorbike battery while rolling down a hill and releasing the clutch in second gear. Another beautiful lesson that came out stranding myself. I'll be ready next time!

Let's look at how this plays out in society with two concepts we generally perceive as bad: death and struggle. What happens when we change our stories around death?

Death is a taboo topic—especially in Western culture. We'll watch slasher films with bloody bodies all over the place, but confront our own mortality? No thanks, too morbid. Life is good. Death is bad.

Our gods are immortal. Our heroes, seemingly invincible, often survive the deadliest of feats. Our celebrities are ageless beauties. From birth to old age, our society tells us to avoid aging and to fear death. Women, especially, can be robbed of realizing the radiant wisdom that comes with the passage of time because youth, we believe, is good.

We lament our wrinkles, trick knees, and grey hair. Visiting a hospital or nursing home where our cherished elders are left to eat bland food in front of melodramatic daytime television makes us uncomfortable. Perhaps that's because we see our own future.

When a celebrity dies, it feels too close for comfort, like somehow we thought they'd escape. But it provides a flash of insight: no matter where we come from or what we've accomplished in life, death comes for all of us. It is the great equalizer. Indeed, even "good" people die.

If death is the final rite of passage on our Hero's Journey, I wonder why we don't become better friends with it early on. Is there any value in asking, "What if I were to die tomorrow?" I mean, asking and really allowing yourself to go there, not just giving lip service to what has become a clichéd question we're asked by country songs and Instagram memes. What would you do differently? Why wait until death is imminent to fully live?

I actually don't think it's death that scares us the most. It's our fear of not fully living. Death is just a reminder that our time on earth is finite. When our perception of death is purely negative, we miss the beautiful opportunities it can give us. We don't see the whole story. These opportunities might come wrapped in uncomfortable packages, but unpacking and reframing the predicaments we put ourselves in reveals the beauty and symmetry of life.

Memento mori is a Latin phrase that means "remember that you will die." The Stoic philosophers used this conscious awareness of impending death as a reminder to treat each day as a gift. Instead of running from death, the Stoics welcomed it into their daily consciousness in order to live a meaningful life. Steve Jobs embraced this philosophy, which he eloquently expressed as part of his 2005 Stanford University commencement address:

> Remembering that I'll be dead soon is the most important tool I've ever encountered to help me make the big choices in life. Almost everything—all external expectations, all pride, all fear of embarrassment or failure—these things just fall away in the face of death, leaving only what is truly important. Remembering that you are going to die is the best way I know to avoid the trap of thinking you have something to lose. You are already naked. There is no reason not to follow your heart.

Of course, most of us don't want to die, but that's different from a fear of dying or perceiving death as purely negative. Our hardwired survival instinct exists alongside our curiosity to uncover new truths about ourselves and test the boundaries of our existence. We don't simply want to survive. We want to thrive, but thriving doesn't come without struggle, without pushing our limits.

If nobody gets out alive, why not take those big, scary risks? Why not push your limits to see what's possible? Author Hunter S. Thompson wrote, "Life should not be a journey to the grave with the intention of arriving safely in a pretty and well-preserved body, but rather to skid in broadside in a cloud of smoke, thoroughly used up, totally worn out, and loudly proclaiming 'Wow! What a Ride!'"

We need to change the narrative that death and struggle are always bad. Just like the story about good and bad luck, it takes a shift in perspective. Instead of forcing one idea, we can choose to explore the other. While we're at it, let's debunk the idea that if we're not good at something, we should give up.

Billy Oppenheimer of the *Six and 6* blog highlights some of the most talented creators alive today, reminding us that success comes from our ability to stick with something and keep working on it even if it's bad. Multi-Grammy-Award-winning producer Rick Rubin says, "Everything is bad for a while before it gets good."

The struggle, the falling down, it's all part of the process. To write a hit song, you have to write a hundred flops. You won't excel at something unless you're willing to be bad at it. Oppenheimer includes a quote from Randall Stutman, founder of Admired Leadership, who says, "You're only as good as you're willing to be bad."

In a similar vein, my good friend Jaemin Frazer says the secret to living a successful and fulfilled life is having more bad days. Not making room for slip-ups means your identity is wrapped up in needing to look, be, and act good all the time. You must always be at the top of your game. A bad day, week, or (heaven forbid) year must mean there's something wrong with you.

But if things are always good, you never really know what "good" is. You need to experience bad to understand good. The sting of the cold gifts us with the comfort of warmth. The pain of heartbreak teaches us the value of love. The acceptance of death allows us to fully live life.

During the 2010 Winter Olympics, which were held in my home city of Vancouver, Slovenian cross-country skier Petra Majič made headlines with her ability to push the limits of her pain tolerance. During her warm-up, she slipped and plummeted a full ten feet into a rocky creek. Unbeknownst to her, she'd broken five ribs, and one was piercing her lung.

Before going to the hospital owing to, you know, the excruciating pain of broken ribs, she skied through four rounds of competition and won a bronze medal. Her mental toughness and willingness to go to the absolute edges of her pain tolerance inspired millions—myself included. The whole Achilles' heel story aside, I have purposely put myself in challenging situations, like trailblazing in the northern wilderness of British Columbia, somehow evading grizzlies and fighting off hypothermia.

I'll spare you the gruesome, black-toed and blistery details, but I deliberately did it to push my limits, to explore the boundaries of my perceived edges, and to see what I was capable of. When I came out the other side, those self-imposed limits laughed in my face.

These intentional, limit-pushing endeavors are called *misogis*, after the Shinto water-cleansing and purification ritual that people undergo by standing under a waterfall. Dr. Marcus Elliot is a physician specializing in performance enhancement and the development of elite athletes. He, along with a few others, have popularized the concept. Elliot says, "A *misogi* is not about physical accomplishment. But rather what we are willing to put ourselves through, mentally and spiritually, to be a better human."

Jesse Itzler, entrepreneur, former rapper, and husband of Spanx founder Sara Blakely, gives these instructions for *misogi*: "Put one big thing on the calendar that scares you, that you never thought you could do, and go out and do it."

Today, most of us do the opposite. We surround ourselves with comfort and convenience to avoid struggle. But it turns out, we're actually killing ourselves with comfort.

In Michael Easter's book *The Comfort Crisis*, he writes, "We are moving about 14 times less than our ancestors. We spend 95 percent of our time indoors and spend 11 hours and 6 minutes a day engaging with digital media. So, we went from never having this digital media in our lives to now it's essentially become our lives. And that's had consequences for our attention, our awareness, how we spend our time, and also our interactions with others. Things have really changed, and we're too comfortable now."

While writing his book, Easter discovered that 98 percent of people choose short-term comfort over long-term growth. Yes, 98 percent! In the age of ultimate convenience, we are indeed in a comfort crisis. Why? Probably because we've been taught that feeling bad is considered a bad thing. Feeling unsafe is bad. Struggling on your way up the corporate ladder is bad. Being bored is bad. Waiting more than an hour for the pizza delivery is bad. What's good? Comfort, ease, convenience, distraction.

We can order takeout from an app and binge watch just about anything we want on Netflix, Hulu, HBO, Apple TV, or YouTube. Not feeling up for that Zoom meeting? Just say you're having technical issues. When silence is deafening, Spotify will fill the void. Taxes need doing? House need cleaning? Errands need running? There are a zillion podcasts to listen to instead.

Road trips used to mean gathering paper maps, plotting the route, folding the maps the wrong way (how did that always happen?), then asking for directions at a gas station after that inevitable wrong turn. Now we just plug the destination into our phone and some nice lady tells us where to go and even which route is fastest. Yet we scroll through Instagram liking *Life is a journey, not a destination* posts.

Instant gratification is also a popular menu selection. It wasn't long ago that 6–8 weeks for delivery was the norm. Now that timeline has been cut down to a day or two … or even a few hours. The anticipation that used to build, culminating in an enthusiastic "It's here!" upon delivery, is gone. Now we don't even know if the package that shows up has the T-shirts, dish soap, or that book we ordered.

This is not to say modern conveniences are always bad, of course. When used consciously and intentionally, they're great. The problem arises when they become a crutch and a means of distracting ourselves from discomfort, which often stems from what we want to avoid.

Somewhere deep inside, we know better. A little nagging voice tells us to change things up, to push ourselves, to break our comfy convenience routines, to stop with the excuses. That inner wisdom reminds us of who we are and the struggles our ancestors overcame just to stay alive.

These are all lessons I could have used to reframe the stories I told myself when I dropped out of college. Later, when I started to see the good hidden inside the bad (and vice versa), I softened my reaction to all the seemingly good and bad events in my life. Why? Because life's a lot more complicated than it appears.

Whether we choose to or not, we're going to live out the full spectrum of our life experiences, which includes the good, the bad, and the ugly. No one leaves this world without doing something that someone somewhere would label as "bad." We torture ourselves by labeling things as bad when all we need to do is give ourselves permission to change perspectives and show up as ourselves. As they say, *we* get to write our own story.

7

Permission

I hate to advocate drugs, alcohol, violence, or insanity to anyone,
but they've always worked for me.

~ Hunter S. Thompson

Most of us grow up learning to ask for permission—permission to be excused from the dinner table, play outside, use the bathroom, eat a cookie, stay up late, watch TV. The list goes on and on. This is a normal (and necessary) part of growing up, but it becomes so ingrained that we continue asking permission throughout adulthood without even realizing it. To follow our dreams, we ask permission from our parents, our peers, our bosses, institutions.

Good grades early on in school give us permission to continue learning from the best teachers. The best schools give us permission to ask for the best jobs. The best jobs give us permission to buy the best house, and so on. Nope, no societal inequalities or blind spots there!

Receiving permission makes us feel good about ourselves; it's confirmation we're on the so-called right path. But when permission is denied, it can lead us to feel unworthy and undeserving, so we cling even tighter to a controlled, predictable and safe existence. Dreams are abandoned. Lives are half lived. The shadow continues to consume.

When we fear judgement and possible rejection, we revert back to the Mother, May I? game. You know, the one where kids stand shoulder to shoulder and "Mother" calls on one of them to take a giant step forward. That person must then ask, "Mother, may I?" before taking a step; otherwise, they go back to the starting line.

In the game it's clear who the players are seeking permission from: Mother. But in life, who is it? When we wait for permission to take a step forward, who are we asking?

Permission to marry your high school sweetheart
Permission to buy a house
Permission to live on a commune
Permission to join the military
Permission to travel the world

As you now know, from the time I was a teenager, I had an unhealthy relationship with cross-country running and track and field. I didn't even know how I actually felt about the sport most of the time—I was simply exhausted. Rising at dawn, I'd run for miles, then I'd sit in a classroom and fight the urge to drift off for a little snooze before I laced up again in the afternoon.

Running became a source of comfort but also misery. The more I ran, the less of "me" existed outside of it. There was an itch deep in my bones to know more of life, but I felt trapped. I was good at running, so running made me good. Stopping would be very, very bad. That subtext had been written in every conversation since I finished my first quarter mile: Joel is a runner, a very good and promising runner.

But what about that other part of me? I knew it was in there somewhere, yet I didn't know what it was or how to reconcile it with "Joel the runner."

I felt like I had to be an ambassador for running—with all its discipline and hard work—at the expense of everything else.

There is a little bit more to my Achilles story that I'll share with you now.

I didn't feel like I had permission *not* to be a runner, so after injuring my Achilles, forfeiting my scholarship, and returning home to attend community college, I slowly started training again. Soon I was past the aforementioned thirty minutes of slow, purgatorial jogging, and I even started racing a little. Then, about six months after my Achilles injury, I hurt myself again. And then again.

While my body was breaking down, something deeper inside was breaking as well. By the third or fourth injury in eighteen months, I was no longer reaching for the frozen corn, hopping on the stationary bike, or going to the physiotherapist. When people asked how my rehab was going, I'd say it was going just fine. The chronic lying started to scare me.

My new coaches talked of special orthopedics for my shoes and new training regimes, but those words were nothing more than noise. Over the coming months, instead of lacing up my running shoes I immersed myself in books about distant places. That itch for the other part of me needed scratching before I jumped out of my skin. For once I wasn't going to ask permission, and I decided my next run would take me far away.

For the first time in a long time, I did the opposite of "Mother, may I?" Not even my parents knew what I was up to. I was nearly twenty years old and could do what I wanted, but I knew my next move would let everyone down. All those people who had loyally given themselves to me over the years so I could focus on training—I was going to break their hearts.

I summoned enough courage to tell my parents and coaches that I needed an extended break from running, reassuring them I'd be back. Another lie. Throughout my life, the only thing that ever settled the buzzing and stinging of my pre-race nerves was planning our annual family vacation in the arid mountains of Okanagan Valley, British Columbia. Even at nine years old, I'd go to the local travel agency and get the free maps to plan new routes so we could see new things. I'd help pack the family van the night before, and I'd be there when the car was warming up at 5:00 a.m. For one of those trips, my father bought a book about a man who'd hitchhiked across Canada.

On top of my running and schooling, I'd been working a few jobs to save up for something. Saving, I'd been told, was good. And now I was about to spend all of it. My hiking bag was packed and hidden away in my bedroom; my route mapped out. I was going to hitchhike across the country.

A seed deep inside me was about to sprout—into what, I didn't know. I was going to walk through an enigmatic doorway into something entirely new. And in doing so, I would leave behind the security of my suburban life, along with the expectations of my family and society.

My mother definitely didn't see this coming, and she was terrified. It didn't make sense to her, or to anyone else, that I would "give up something I was so good at." And, for the first time, not making sense was actually fine with me. Not seeking approval felt … liberating.

As a dirtbag traveler (that's what that author who inspired my vagabonding called himself), each new town or region I entered promised something new to explore, both externally and internally. I was, once again, that boy exploring the swamp with no dinner bells or school deadlines.

Sleeping in a field just outside the Rockies, I stared up at an expanse of stars and was reminded of the natural beauty and freedom I had completely forgotten.

Racing through a summer storm in the black of night on the side of some long-forgotten highway, I was also reminded of my fragility. It felt mighty good to be a small spec in a vast creation as opposed to the "big fish in a small pond" identity I'd rather arrogantly adopted.

Patiently waiting for my next ride under big prairie skies—the neon glow of cities long gone—I experienced a slowness that my prior restlessness would never allow.

Elation and deflation would sum up my hitchhiking experience.

Kilometer after kilometer, as I walked along Canada's Highway Number 1, I tried to leave my old self behind and discover something new. The pavement caused my feet to ache, the rides being more infrequent than I had imagined. With each approaching car, I hoped—longed even—for a pick-up. And as they passed by without stopping, pangs of judgement and unworthiness shot through me.

Most people were probably scared I'd chop them up into little pieces, and who could blame them? We're wired to protect ourselves. But those feelings of loneliness and rejection made for some pretty dark dialogues with myself. I started to internalize drivers' perceived judgements of who I was—bad, nasty, dangerous, the "other." Those feelings were already there, but each passing car brought them to the surface, and I had nothing but time to ruminate on them. Jon Kabat-Zinn's adage, wherever you go there you are, (meaning you can't run away from your problems) seemed an evil laughing refrain.

Then, just when I couldn't take it any longer, a car would slow down and pull over. My heart would leap, and I'd jog over, sporting a big, reassuring smile that I was no serial killer.

From British Columbia to Alberta, Saskatchewan to Ontario, an interesting thing began to happen. Each new driver who picked me up offered me a chance to be seen for who I was at that moment. I wasn't Joel the runner. I was just a stranger who needed a ride. It was like we were two people dropped from the cosmos into the same metal bucket on four tires to learn something important. All we knew about each other was what we talked about in the car.

There were war veterans, truckers, recent widows, couples on once-in-a-lifetime road trips, and college kids returning home for the summer. Each interaction offered a chance to experience myself without the labels, to see myself through a stranger's eyes. And in their kind eyes, I saw my own goodness.

The people who offered me a ride didn't expect anything from me, except maybe some company for an hour or so. Simply being a human in need of a ride was enough to warrant their kindness and generosity. To receive, all I had to do was to ask and to be present. And what I received was often far more than just a faster way to cover some ground.

I remember somewhere beside a grassy field in the vast Canadian Prairie, I shared why I was hitchhiking with a gentleman kind of enough to give me a ride.

"I just couldn't be there anymore," I told him.

An inviting silence followed, the silence of a person who is genuinely listening. Over the low rumble of the car, I continued.

"There was this girl in college I liked. She was beautiful and I would've loved to ask her out. One night I was with my good friend, and we were talking about her. There was a party that night and she would be there, so my friend suggested we go. But I didn't want to. I didn't really go to parties because eating and drinking late into the night would affect my training routine.

"We had been friends forever, so he didn't hold back on his response, 'This girl likes you but thinks you're no fun. If you don't start going out, you won't have any memories or any experiences worth living for. If you don't take chances, you're never going to get the girl.'

It hurt to hear that, but I felt a greater calling. Like I was going to leave this town and make something of myself. Then people—that girl included—would like and respect me. But there was a small part of me that believed him because I never did go to that party, and that stuck with me . . . Anyway."

I shifted in my seat as we exited the highway onto a little pullout at the edge of the expansive prairie. "Then I got injured and I was really angry about everything I'd missed out on—the parties, the fun, the adventures. Maybe that girl would have liked me, and maybe we could've had something. Anyway, even after my injury, people kept asking me about running. I just couldn't take it anymore.

It's not even that I hate running. But what it's all become . . . I don't even know. It's just . . . a burden. I'm thankful for it. Running taught me how to be comfortable with pain and struggle. It kept me fit. It taught me discipline and how to win. But I'm mad at it at the same time, you know? I hope that makes sense."

He nodded slowly, as if he could see all the mixed-up messiness inside me.

"When I wasn't who everyone thought I was, or wanted me to be, I felt worthless. Maybe they just cared, and it was all in my head, but my head felt like it was going to explode, so I decided to get up and go. It was the first time I ever did something I wanted without asking permission."

The wind rustled the dry grass under the hot sun. The man listened intently and puffed on his cigarette. Then, with kind, almost sad eyes, he gestured to the golden landscape and said, "Son, you are reflected in all of this. Experiencing the world's richness and fullness doesn't require permission. Just action."

I paused, my full attention on him.

He continued, "But I realized that much too late. All the other stuff is just noise."

Silvery smoke escaped the corner of his mouth. "We just become so fixated on ourselves, trying to get things right, that we complicate the hell out of it."

That landed pretty hard. As the days and weeks passed during my travels, I realized that I really did love running. It wasn't the high of winning or the progressive improvement; it was the mind-body connection of running over hill and dale. Running free, without asking for permission, and experiencing the extent of my power and my breath when I ran fast. I felt wild and alive, like I was that boy again back in the swamp. But I couldn't tap into this when I ran competitively.

Far past the borders of Canada I ran. Asia called me next. Then Central and South America. At the edges of our world, I searched for the edges of myself. New people, strange foods, and foreign cultures opened the doorway to my soul. I lost and found myself over and over again, creating more distance between who I actually was and who I was supposed to be.

I would remember that man's words, feeling the reciprocal relationship between the world and myself, where I was absorbing it and it was absorbing me. I slowly let go of who I thought I needed to be in favor of simply being. No labels, no judgement. Just breathing life in and breathing it out.

I gave myself permission to crash against life, to let out a primal, unbound scream at the top of a mountain; to dance all night without wondering what people thought of me; to shock my body in icy waters; to lose myself in lustful, anonymous one-night stands.

My buddy would've been proud of all the experiences I collected.

I felt like a character in a Jack Kerouac novel… that is until I returned home.

Back at home, I reverted to old habits. Thank you, Mr. Kabat-Zinn, for your perpetually frustrating reminder that life continues to present us with the same lessons until we actually learn them. I replaced running races with running businesses, still believing my worth was tied to success. I hung up my racing spikes for good and moved to New York City to grow an underwear company I'd started called Naked, trading my runner label for the entrepreneur label. This is known as transference: "Transference is when someone redirects their feelings about one person onto someone else." We do it with things, too, redirecting our feelings about one thing onto something else. Although I didn't realize it at the time, I was just chasing different wins. And once again there was a disconnect between who I wanted to be and who I was showing up as.

Enter self-discrepancy theory.

Psychology professor and researcher Dr. E. Tory Higgins developed self-discrepancy theory in the 1980s. It suggests there are three different self-domains: the "actual self" (how a person perceives himself/herself to actually be), the "ought self" (how a person should be according to societal norms or duties), and the "ideal self" (who a person aspires to be).

According to the theory, when there is a conflict or discrepancy between the actual and ideal self, disappointment, dissatisfaction, and sadness result because outcomes fall short of what the person idealized (absence of a positive outcome). When there is a discrepancy between the actual and ought selves, fear and restlessness can result because outcomes fall short of someone else's expectations (presence of a negative outcome).

I struggled with both conflicts. Earlier in life, I needed to be what other people expected of me: a good runner, enthusiastic student, and model son. So, I lived that "ought" existence instead of asking myself what I really wanted.

Later, I moved into the actual–ideal self-conflict, holding myself to ridiculous standards in business, partnership, and parenthood. When my business failed, a story shared in great detail in my first book *Getting Naked*, I saw myself falling short in every area of life, and old feelings of inadequacy came roaring back.

Finding myself in this familiar and unwanted place again, I decided it was time for another journey, one that would take me deeper into myself than I had ever been and force me to feel the breadth of emotions I'd been suppressing for so long.

For that level of emotional release to be possible, I had to learn to let go and separate myself from ego, something I felt required help from an ancient remedy, one with mystical properties.

8

Emotion

If I create from the heart, nearly everything works;
if from the head, almost nothing.

~ Marc Chagall

As we discussed previously, in today's world of distraction, comfort, and convenience, choosing *not* to feel is easier than ever. We scroll through social media, go down internet rabbit holes (why *are* all the bees dying?), watch TV, stay perpetually busy, clean the house—anything to avoid negative or unwanted emotions.

A glass of scotch takes the edge off. A THC gummy calms frayed nerves. A carton of fudge ripple ice cream trades sadness for pleasure . . . if only for a moment. By constantly numbing our pain, we end up sleepwalking through life in a quasi-zombie state.

Instead of accepting negative emotions as a part of the human experience, we put a positive spin on things, no matter how dire or tragic. It's called toxic positivity. Since positive feelings are "good" and negative feelings are "bad," toxic positivity tells us to selectively choose the positive ones. Like my friends encouraging me to look on the bright side at a time when one of my businesses was going under (I'll spare you the gruesome details). They meant well, of course, but their advice invalidated my actual and present feelings of embarrassment, worthlessness, and defeat.

This brand of positive thinking doesn't work because you can't decide which emotions you want to feel. If you numb pain, you also numb joy. If you avoid negative emotions, you block yourself from the positive ones too. This suppression can lead to self-judgement, shame, and even deeper feelings of inadequacy. It strengthens our shadow self.

Despite society's affinity for oversimplified, polarized thinking, two opposite emotions can exist at the same time. In fact, holding space for both is exactly the point of this book. Bittersweet is a word we use to describe situations that are both happy and sad. Life transitions are full of them: moving to a new house, a child going off to college, retirement. When one thing comes to an end, something new begins.

It's possible to be happy for someone else's success while you're sad about your own situation. You can be hurt by someone and also proud of yourself for expressing your feelings. You can regret a choice you made and still be excited about the opportunities ahead. Unfortunately, society has conditioned us to believe we have to choose one or the other. We don't.

It's the emotional equivalent of having your cake and eating it too.

A research study involving more than 11,000 participants reported that, on average, people experienced at least one emotion 90 percent of the time and that they simultaneously experienced positive and negative emotions relatively frequently. How many different emotions do we experience? Researchers can't quite agree.

In the 1970s, psychologist Paul Eckman identified six basic emotions: happiness, sadness, fear, disgust, surprise, and anger. Then, in 2017, UC

Berkeley's Greater Good Science Center conducted a study that revealed at least twenty-seven emotions. In 2021, Brené Brown published her book *Atlas of the Heart*, in which she describes eighty-seven. Like our continual discovery of new species in the Amazon, it seems the more we research emotions, the more we uncover.

Regardless of which words you use to describe how you feel, naming your emotions can help you process them. If you say, "I'm disappointed in myself," or "I'm afraid of what people will think of me," or "I'm devastated by what just happened," you give those feelings permission to exist. Journaling and talking to someone (a friend, therapist, coach) are good outlets for identifying those feelings.

Do this regularly, and you'll be better equipped to handle the range of swirling emotions we humans experience. The irony is, the sooner you acknowledge your barrage of emotions and allow them in, the faster they will disappear. As much as we fear being sucked into the abyss, when we actively feel our feelings and identify what they are, we don't stay down there very long.

And now, dear reader, it's time to explore something mystical in the pursuit of identifying and feeling suppressed emotions. For this we go to the Amazon. Not in search of rare insects or giant anacondas, but of powerful plants.

I was lying on a thin yoga mat in pitch darkness surrounded by fifteen other people. The bittersweet taste of the medicine lingered on my tongue as I questioned my mental state—was I awake or in a lucid dream? Soon (I think it was soon, though I had no concept of time), I transcended into profound nothingness where my ego disappeared entirely. I was in the arms of Mother Ayahuasca.

In this expanded consciousness, I became an observer, like watching myself on a movie screen. I felt completely separate from my thoughts while simultaneously feeling connected to nature, other people, creativity, peace. Everything I had piled onto myself—expectations, blame, shame, unworthiness—vaporized. With this shift in perspective, my true self came into focus.

Ayahuasca and other psychedelic substances like LSD, mescaline, psilocybin (magic mushrooms), and DMT trigger mental, visual, and auditory changes that produce an altered or expanded state of consciousness, a state where both euphoria and paranoia are common. Many indigenous cultures refer to these compounds as spiritual medicine. When ingested therapeutically and under the supervision of a trained administrator, they can lead to transformational healing.

Author Michael Pollan is a leading investigator of the scientific use of LSD and psilocybin to provide relief from addiction, PTSD, depression, and anxiety. He explains: "The drugs foster new perspectives on old problems. You know, one of the things our mind does is tell stories about ourselves. And if you're depressed, you're being told a story, perhaps, that you're worthless, that no one, you know, could possibly love you; you're not worthy of love, that life will not get better. And these stories, which are enforced by our egos, really, trap us in these ruminative loops that are very hard to get out of."

Spiritual medicines can help you get out of them. I learned about Ayahuasca on my travels and discussed its healing powers with people I was close to—people I trusted. Contrary to their recent rise in popularity, these are not novel remedies. Research shows that psychedelic substances like mushrooms have been used in shamanic practices dating back to 5000 B.C., so these substances, and the sacred ceremonies around them, are highly respected and revered.

For me, it seemed impossible to make those old habits die hard, and I approached the Ayahuasca experience more like Joel "the runner" than Joel "the dirtbag traveler." I prepared for my medicine journey for two full years before the actual Ayahuasca experience, all the while working with a professional counselor and shaman. First, I participated in a ceremony with cacao, then another with low dose psilocybin as an easing in process to become acquainted with different rituals and the deep inward journeys that accompany them.

To prepare for the physical challenges of an Ayahuasca ceremony, I sat in a sweat lodge with a First Nations elder. Each participant had a role in preparing for the sweat (a common physical side effect of Ayahuasca). Some helped build the fire while others made tea, then the ancestors were called to join us. When the fire was reduced to embers, we all sat in the intense heat and pitch darkness in what I can only describe as being steamed alive.

Each round of four sweats lasted fifteen minutes, and the intermittent relief of the cool winter air outside felt like a giant gasp of oxygen after being submerged under water. This experience, like the other ceremonies, also elicited a deep inner journey where I battled mental and physical demons. After another six months of breath practice and meditation, I was finally ready to meet Mother Ayahuasca.

Ayahuasca is an entheogenic brew made primarily from the *Banisteriopsis caapi* vine that grows in the Amazon basin. Many, believing it represents the feminine energy, refer to Ayahuasca as La Madre, the Grandmother, the Lady, or Mother Aya. She's also known as the Purge, because vomiting, diarrhea, sweating, and crying are often part of the cleansing process.

Three weeks prior to the ceremony, I adopted a strict diet: no spices, alcohol, caffeine, pork, or refined sugar. I also had to abstain from sex, news, violent shows, and social media. Some people fast for twenty-four hours to limit vomiting. I didn't go quite that far, but I ate very little.

Our small group was guided through the ceremony by a shaman and other trained practitioners. A strict vow of silence allowed us to turn inward and freely explore what was happening without fear of judgement. Before the ceremony, we set clear intentions about what we wanted to get out of the experience. I wanted to heal my feeling of "badness" and get off the hedonic treadmill. I hoped to unearth old wounds and heal them in a way I had been unable to fully accomplish on my own.

The ceremony included ingesting the Ayahuasca tea, chanting, singing, drumming, journaling, and focusing on our intentions. Whenever the shaman caught me enjoying the warmth of the sunshine or staring at the trees, she came over to work with me. She challenged me to go inward and focus on the healing I sought, and to sit with myself and with all the emotions that surfaced.

Many factors can affect your experience, such as how much love the shaman projects to you and the people you're with, the music selection, the chants, the dancing, the breathing, the intention you set. All of it is part of healing. Here is my experience, as clearly as I can explain something that was unlike anything I had experienced before.

I am back in my old childhood bedroom that fateful night of my pre-race meltdown. I see myself in bed crying, my well-intentioned mother standing next to me, at a loss for how to comfort her son. I clearly see two humans sharing an enormous amount of pain and fear. I feel deep compassion for this child and his mother. The unworthiness and anxiety I felt at the time is absent. They are abstract ideas, non-existent in this new world.

A "knowing" wells up in me. Any failure is simply part of the human experience. I had a choice, and I always have a choice, in how I feel and how I respond to it. Then things zoom out and I see both of my parents—not their physical state but their essence—creating me out of love and goodness. I witness this uncomplicated creation that is as close to God's unconditional love as I can comprehend. I don't use the word *God* here in a religious sense, only to express the utmost pinnacle of love that exists in this world. I see myself as a tiny piece in a giant puzzle, which makes my "bad" decisions feel less significant in the overall scheme of things.

Then, I find myself by a lake I had run next to many times. Still as glass, the lake is surrounded by lush evergreens—and I have it all to myself. I walk into the cool water. I feel reborn. Eventually, I make my way to the soft, moist ground. There I experience the kind of love you have for a child when you first meet them, knowing nothing of their personality, temperament, or goodness. This is the bedrock of love from which we all come, a love that doesn't care about who I am or what I've done. My ego, which would dismiss this as complete nonsense, is dead and gone.

This feeling moves through me. I weep so deeply I'm shaking. Every tear I never cried but wanted to comes through me now. Tears of immense sadness. Tears of hot anger. Tears of regret and disappointment. Then, I laugh through tears of joy. I wasted all that time feeling bad: losing that race at age fifteen, dropping out of school, the virginity debacle, a failed business, disappointing my parents more times than I can count.

I laugh at the ridiculousness of my addiction to work and my attachment to success. I am in stitches thinking about the time I wasted comparing myself to people whose lives I wanted. My obsession with amassing credit card points and air miles catapults me even deeper into hysterics.

This unguarded laughter is profoundly healing—and revealing. I see theabsurdity in all of it. Why do I seek so much approval? What am I afraid of? Why do I ask permission to be myself?

At the end of the ceremony, we all shared our experience and what we learned, and the shaman provided insights into what we didn't understand. Although I felt like I'd just breezed through ten years of psychotherapy in one evening, I wasn't so naive as to believe my ego wouldn't come roaring back with its demands once the halo had worn off.

The use of ancient rituals and hallucinogens to experience expanded states of consciousness might not sit well with some people. I get it, and although I'm not evangelizing the use of psychedelics or spiritual medicine, I gave myself permission to explore them.*

By suppressing my ego and muzzling the judgmental critic in my head, I experienced the full, unedited expression of my emotions. From painful to joyful, feelings I had shoved down since childhood came spilling out in a cathartic release.

In contrast, invalidating emotions by shoving them into a corner, putting a positive spin on them, numbing, distracting ourselves, can all turn us into human pressure cookers. This played out in my need to pack up and leave it all behind—which, of course, doesn't work in the long run. If you give those feelings space to be felt when they come up, you slowly release the pressure. Continue to suppress them, however, and explosions can happen at the most inopportune times.

Remember how ski resorts induce mini avalanches to prevent giant, more destructive ones? The same can be done with emotions. By processing them little by little instead of letting those negative feelings accumulate, you can avoid an unscheduled, out-of-control avalanche.

Years ago, a work colleague lost her dad. She always acted very professional,

---

* Practitioners I've worked with cannot stress enough the significance, seriousness, and sacredness of the medicine. They do not view these experiences as recreation—they should not be. These substance are illegal in many parts of the world and taking any psychotropic compound that affects brain chemistry should be approached with extreme caution, especially for those with a history of psychosis, PTSD, or bipolar disorders (Terry Gross, "'Reluctant Psychonaut' Michael Pollan Embraces 'New Science' of Psychedelics," *Fresh Air*, NPR, May 24, 2019, https://www.wbfo.org/2019-05-24/reluctant-psychonaut-michael-pollan-embraces-new-science-of-psychedelics).

and so I never saw her grief around the office. Then, during a presentation, a client asked an innocuous question and her eyes watered. She shook her head to stem the tears, but they flowed anyways, and she had to excuse herself from the presentation. I felt terrible for her.

Sudden and uncontrollable emotions can show us where we still need to heal. Processing negative feelings requires practice; however, from a young age, that skill is often beaten out of us by our parents, by our culture, and by society.

Stop crying.
Chin up.
Don't be a baby.
Look on the bright side.
Be strong.
Everything happens for a reason.
Happiness is a choice.
Stay positive.
You shouldn't feel that way.

One night my wife and I were visiting friends for dinner and their daughter had a massive meltdown. After she wiped her swollen eyes and then ran to her bedroom, we got the full story from her parents.

She often came home from school, lost her iPad privileges for something she'd done, and then completely broke down. Initially, they thought it was just a spoiled kid having a temper tantrum, so they put their "bad" kid in counseling to "fix" her.

But, to their surprise, these meltdowns had nothing to do with what was happening at the moment (i.e., not being able to use her iPad). Rather, they were a release of pent-up emotions from a long day at school being on her best behavior and not allowed to act out or express her feelings. A small 'no,' like a screentime restriction was enough to push the emotional floodgates wide open.

The counselor suggested our friends encourage their daughter to "go to the feeling" while reassuring her of their love and providing a safe space for her to express herself without fear of judgement. Another tactic our friends used was to allow their daughter's emotions to naturally come out in play. They learned that if she threw her doll off a pretend cliff, it was not a morbid act, but a healthy one. It was a way to deal with her feelings, not a sign she might set the house on fire!

"Adaptation comes from feeling," according to Dr. Deborah Mac in her parenting book *Rest, Play, Grow*. "Don't mask your child's emotions with candy or video games just to make it stop. Otherwise, she won't learn to adapt." A warm reminder for my own parenting.

But when temper tantrums lead to punishment and when misbehaving earns the label of *bad kid*, it's no wonder we grow up learning to suppress our feelings. Our experience tells us it's not safe to express them. It's better to sit still, be "good," and pretend everything is fine.

As a society, we practice this nearly every day:

"Hey, how are you?"

"Good, how are you?"

"I'm fine, thanks."

Of course, you wouldn't launch into a diatribe about your stressful morning or your mom's declining health to someone you pass in the hallway, but repeatedly answering a question with an inauthentic answer normalizes the suppression of emotion. It's not only culturally acceptable to hide how we're feeling, it's expected.

This can morph into shielding ourselves from pain and discomfort. During my primary school years, whenever the teacher called on me, my cheeks would flush, my brow would sweat, and I'd feel dizzy, like I was going to pass out:

"Joel, please read this off the chalkboard."
"Joel, please come up here and write this down."

I'm dyslexic, so going up and writing a word backwards or (even worse) spelling it wrong in front of the entire class could result in death by peer laughter. But I could never let these feelings show; that would result in even more humiliation, so I stuffed my terror down. Later, even in a more mature, free-thinking university classroom, I still recall the soul-sucking humiliation of a pronunciation blunder that I made during my sophomore year.

To illustrate what my friends and colleagues now call a Joel-ism, I once famously blurted façade as "*faa-kaide*"—and on a podcast no less!

To say something correctly and coherently out loud, I needed to practice it at least twice in my head. As for writing, I adopted a doctor's style of illegible handwriting so no one could tell if I misspelled something. Why invite failure or heartbreak or humiliation and shame into your life if you don't have to?

If you aren't confronted with something that might make you angry, sad, disappointed, anxious, or any other "negative" emotion, you can avoid those feelings altogether. Your world gets smaller and smaller because the risk of doing something that might bring incredible joy isn't worth the potential pain. This is one path to unfulfilling jobs, relationships, and lives in general. You may not raise your hand for an emotionless existence, but every time you suppress your feelings or avoid situations that could lead to uncomfortable emotions, you take one more step in that direction.

James Clear, author of *Atomic Habits: An Easy & Proven Way to Build Good Habits & Break Bad Ones*, puts it this way: "Every action you take is a vote for the type of person you wish to become. No single instance will transform your beliefs, but as the votes build up, so does the evidence of your new identity. This is one reason why meaningful change does not require radical change. Small habits can make a meaningful difference by providing evidence of a new identity. And if a change is meaningful, it is actually big. That's the paradox of making small improvements."

Yes, you can create a habit of feeling your emotions. For example, if you wake up on the wrong side of the bed, don't just get up and go about your day. Acknowledge how you're feeling and try to name it. Are you *sad, depressed, frustrated, anxious, stressed*? Then give yourself a few minutes to feel it. Even if you don't know the cause, allowing the emotion to surface builds the habit of feeling over avoiding feeling.

Triggering experiences offer opportunities as well. When I snap at my wife or daughters about something, it's a chance for me to reflect on what's happening at a deeper level. Just like our friends' daughter's response to having her iPad taken away, it's rarely about what's happening at the moment. Those emotional reactions point to something deeper inside that hasn't fully healed. Now that I'm aware of this, I am much better able to identify those feelings and openly express what's going on.

You can't heal your emotions if you can't feel them. And negative emotions aren't bad. They're part of being human and they deserve our attention. They are nutrients for the garden of our soul, nourishing it, replenishing it, keeping it alive. When you suppress them, or latch onto one for too long without releasing it, it can spoil the harvest, just as too much sun or not enough water does.

Pema Chödrön, Buddhist nun and author says, "Feelings like disappointment, embarrassment, irritation, resentment, anger, jealousy, and fear, instead of being bad news, are actually very clear moments that teach us where it is that we're holding back. They teach us to perk up and lean in when we feel we'd rather collapse and back away. They're like messengers that show us, with terrifying clarity, exactly where we're stuck. This very moment is the perfect teacher and, lucky for us, it's with us wherever we are."

I believe we transform our lives by exploring the full expression of our emotions. This I now know on a deeply personal level to be true. That being said, we don't always need ego-bending mystical journeys to connect with our feelings. More often small, intentional avalanches will do. In each precious moment is the opportunity to connect with our whole emotional selves—the good and the bad—without judgement. This is how we coax our shadow closer and get to know it. We may not like what we see, but it's part of us.

Acknowledging our "badness" and feeling the weighty emotions that come with it are huge steps toward healing, but that's not the end of the road. To remove the limitations that hold us back, we must fully embrace our shadow and show it unconditional love. And it just so happens there's a tool for that.

9

Forgiveness

Forgiveness is the fragrance that the violet sheds
on the heel that has crushed it.

~ Mark Twain

A friend of mine once told me about the day he found out his wife was having an affair. It had been happening on and off with the same man throughout most of their marriage. Devastated upon hearing his wife's confession, he fell to the floor and painfully gasped for air, his body cold with pain, shock, and anger.

Sometime later that day, while still very much in this state, a higher power called him to give his wife a massage. In a calm whisper he asked his wife, who was still weeping on the floor, to lie on the bed with him. Surprised and grief-stricken, she agreed. For the next hour he gave her a gentle, loving massage, then they both fell peacefully asleep. Embedded in his touch was forgiveness.

As my friend recounted the story to me, I asked what compelled him to do this. He said that, as devastated as he was, he knew she felt just as bad. For whatever pain he felt, he knew she was also in pain. For whatever unworthiness he felt for being cheated on, she also must have felt deep unworthiness for being unfaithful without leaving him.

He knew that if he did not show her, at the zenith of their collective grief and anguish, that she was worthy of love and forgiveness despite what had happened, her shame and guilt may have filled her so deeply that she would never forgive herself. What felt too painful to utter, his massage tenderly communicated.

That was one of the most compassionate and forgiving acts I had ever heard firsthand. In his darkest moment, while experiencing his own devastating pain, he was simultaneously present for hers. And forgiving wasn't just a gift for his wife; it also freed him from being stuck in a cycle of anger, blame, and resentment. By his own account, he had not yet begun to process the full spectrum of emotions; however, stepping into his intention to forgive eased some of his anguish.

According to a study published in the *Journal of Health Psychology*, "developing a more forgiving coping style may help minimize stress-related disorders." Further, the impact of forgiveness has positive benefits on the cardiovascular system and blood pressure."

Forgiveness happens on a continuum. It is both a process and a practice that takes time. Moreover, as our young children often remind us, it is not likely our first impulse. Blame—the sinister sister of forgiveness—usually is.

That's because when we're focused on our own ego, there isn't much space for empathy, compassion, and forgiveness. When it's all about us, we double down on blame, victimhood, and self-righteousness: "How could you do that to me? What kind of person are you? I would *never* do that!"

But again, it's folly to think the spotlight is only on us. That's the ego keeping the shadow at bay. Why? Because deep inside we know we have the capacity to hurt others and acknowledging this capacity would mean accepting our own darkness. I've literally watched one of my daughters baselessly slap the other one across the face and proceed to blame her victim.

Blame is a handy weapon to avoid the truth in ourselves, and it's an ancient one. When God asked Adam what happened in the Garden of Eden, Adam was quick to point the finger at Eve. When Eve was asked, she blamed the serpent.

Back when I left university, forfeiting my scholarship, I blamed my coach at the university and my coach back home for my decision because I was filled with so much shame. I didn't want to be labeled as a bad student, a bad athlete . . . a bad *anything*. Not only did I lack the emotional intelligence to process my feelings, I also didn't know how to forgive myself for making a decision I actually *wanted* to make.

I disappointed a lot of people, something I had tried my entire childhood to avoid. Frankly—and savor the irony here—it was my choice to leave them disappointed. This is where blame cuts two ways. I disappointed myself and others close to me by wielding the weapon of blame instead of being honest.

Most of us have been scarred by something that happened in our childhood, wounds inflicted by our parents or other kids. But instead of blaming them, healing comes from forgiveness. If you have children, you probably tell them not to blame others. Do you follow your own advice?

We think blame lets us off the hook. If it's someone else's fault, there's nothing we need to do. That may seem like a pretty good deal, but it's actually an excuse to stay stuck, unable to move forward. By taking responsibility, you get to call the shots.

I blamed my parents for "making me" run. It wasn't until I realized I'd made a *choice* to run and a *choice* to leave school that the path ahead started to open up. If those were *my* decisions, that meant I was in control of my life and could make other decisions—ones I actually wanted.

When I was sixteen, I spent a lot of time with Ian, a former Olympic cross-country skier from Scotland who served as my mentor. Cross-country skiing is one of the most intense endurance sports out there, and being an Olympic athlete comes with its own pressures, so Ian had a lot of wisdom to impart. And he wasn't into shortcuts; he was a "teach someone to fish" kind of guy.

One night while we sipped tea in his kitchen, Ian asked me a very pointed question, "What do you think it means about you, Joel, if you lose a race?"

He knew I was competitive—that was obvious—but he seemed to sense something deeper at play, and he wanted to help me work through it.

Tongue-tied, I couldn't give him an answer. Maybe because it felt so complicated. Intellectually, I knew losing didn't mean anything. We learn from our losses, after all, and failure, when positively applied, can inform future actions; it can help us improve. I knew that. And I knew my parents would love me even if I lost. Again, this was an intellectual kind of knowing. But deep down, on an emotional level, I didn't believe any of that.

To help me figure out what my emotional self had to say, Ian suggested I go home, close my eyes, and sit in silence. Only when I was feeling relaxed, he said, could I mentally journey back to the moment when I began to believe that my goodness and self-worth were attached to winning.

Maybe then, I would forgive the people who instilled that belief in me and forgive myself for believing it.

Always eager to find an edge that might improve my running, I took Ian up on his advice and parked myself on the floor in the corner of my bedroom, sitting cross-legged like it was "circle reading time" back in kindergarten and wishing the lock on my door actually worked. Back then, it wasn't unusual for a school friend to pop in, and I couldn't imagine the humiliation I would endure if someone walked in on me meditating.

Seated there in quiet solitude, I went back to the raw, anxiety-ridden initiation of my very first race, when every nerve in my body was electrified—and yet I felt paralyzed with fear.

"Nerves are good for you," my mother had said while I was hiding some-where behind the starting line, puking up her cooking, wondering what on earth could be "good" about this (the nerves not the cooking, that is). Winning provided relief, not elation, where I could drain the remaining contents of my stomach somewhere private and then get ready to do it all again the next week.

I know, boo-hoo, right? This guy is complaining about being born fast and having a parent that only wanted the best for him. It's true, on the one hand. Looking back now, I can see how normal and seemingly inconsequential these running-related traumas were. On the other hand, I can't deny the experience that young boy felt. Comparing the severity of our pain and struggle with others' is a senseless and destructive exercise. Trauma isn't a game to be won. If it was, it would be zero sum. Neither, for that matter, is forgiveness. Trauma, blame, and forgiveness are ours and ours alone.

Thankfully, no friends barged in on my first real meditation session, which gave me a sore ass and knees from sitting for so long but was chock-full of insights. First, I realized there might actually be something to this "sitting awkwardly in silence" thing as I felt relaxed and clear-minded after the exercise. I also felt an inkling of forgiveness toward my mother and toward myself for enduring those (literally) gut-wrenching nerves. I felt grateful for what running gave me.

As much as I weep for the boy who wanted to splash around the swamp more than he wanted to run around a track like he was chasing his own tail, I'm grateful for that boy's commitment to the work, and his determination to endure, to compete, and to challenge himself in ways that were patently uncomfortable.

It would be twenty more years before I fully integrated that one session's lesson, but the seed of forgiveness and its healing powers had taken root in me.

The idea of forgiveness wasn't foreign to me, however. I have, believe it or not, my loathed Sunday School to thank for that, although most of the lessons didn't fully stick because I was daydreaming about playing outside instead of actively listening. One that I do remember is the story of the prodigal son, which appears in the Book of Luke. It's pretty well-known, but here's a quick refresher:

> A man has two sons, and the younger one asks for his inheritance early. The father agrees, so the son takes his share and goes to live extravagantly in a foreign land. He squanders it all away and is left desperately poor just as a famine hits. Taking a job tending pigs to survive, he realizes the servants who worked for his father were far better off than he is now, so he journeys home to ask his father for one of those jobs. Admitting his sins, he acknowledges he no longer has the right to be recognized as his father's son. But instead of giving him a servant's job, the father accepts him back into the household with open arms, throwing a lavish party to celebrate his son's return.

I felt like that wayward son many times, and although I desperately wanted to be welcomed back with open arms wherever I had fouled up, I didn't believe I deserved it. I thought forgiveness had to be earned . . . by being good, of course. I didn't know it could be freely given and received, but that's the magic of forgiveness: it's always available. No strings attached.

A modern-day example of forgiveness in action is Father Gregory Boyle, a Catholic priest who became the pastor of Dolores Mission Church in East Los Angeles in 1986. At the time, that community had the highest concentration of gang activity in Los Angeles—a city already known as the gang capital of the world.

In his book *Forgive Everyone Everything*, Boyle writes, "There's no denying how difficult things can be. But the way out to the place of resilience, the place of restoration, the place of not allowing your heart to be hardened by resentment, relies on one thing: forgive everyone everything."

To help those in his community, Boyle founded Homeboy Industries, the largest gang intervention, rehab, and reentry program in the world. In addition to counseling, tattoo removal, tutoring, and substance abuse support, Homeboy Industries operates several social enterprise businesses to support gang-involved and previously incarcerated people by providing employment and job training programs.

Homeboy Bakery, established in 1992, was the first, where rival gang members would work side-by-side and literally break bread together. It's also where these individuals' shadows came out of the darkness to greet each other. Now Homeboy Industries opens its doors to approximately ten thousand gang members every year, offering hope, healing, and second chances.

Jorge Dominguez, a Homeboy employee and graduate of the IT training program, said, "Homeboy is . . . to me, everything. It's my place where I've grown, it's my place where I've been accepted for who I am—the real who I am—it's been a place where I've been accepted for all of my character defects, it's been a place where I eat $2.00 meals because it's affordable. I have my friends who are all from here. Training: I get it here. Therapy: I get it here. Support for school: I get it here. And sometimes, just a hug from people who support you with their hearts . . . I get everything. So, to me, Homeboy is everything."

Isn't it interesting how the forgiveness that's been extended to this young man and the chance to be different going forward provide him with so many of his basic needs and help him evolve as a person? "To not," as the writers of Ted Lasso said, "be judged by the actions of our weakest moments but, rather, by the strength we show when, and if, we're ever given a second chance."

The pain we experience from mistakes or bad behavior grounds us in humanity and connects us to all those who have lived. When we hold onto it, we wither. When we let go of it, we bloom.

There are many beautiful stories of forgiveness. When we acknowledge that good people can do bad things, we don't conflate behavior with identity. Instead of labeling someone as "bad," we allow room for mistakes—even horrible ones. And when we accept that in others, we can accept it in ourselves.

Here's a poignant story that exemplifies both stoicism and forgiveness.

In 2012, Mary Hedges was at a mall with her son when she was struck by a shopping cart that two teenage boys had hurled over a railing fifty feet above her. Hedges spent weeks in a coma fighting for her life. The injury caused severe brain damage, blindness in one eye, and the amputation of her right foot; yet this is what she said about the two boys: "I wish them well, I do. I feel very sorry for them."

Another potent story of forgiveness is from the book *The More Beautiful World Our Hearts Know Is Possible* about Christian Bethelson, a Liberian warlord who went by the *nom de guerre* General Leopard. He seized children and forced them to become soldiers in an unspeakably brutal civil war. If anyone is beyond redemption, it would be him. After the war was over, he was on his way to another country to ply his trade of killing when his vehicle got stuck in the mud. Also stuck was a vehicle carrying members of a peace group, the Everyday Gandhis. He told them who he was, expecting them to beat and punish him, but instead they hugged him and told him they loved him. Last I heard, Bethelson had become a peace worker himself.

The critical step to forgiveness, acceptance, and all acts of healing is awareness, and that needs an acknowledgement of what's happening in our body, mind, relationships, and world. Can you simply pay more attention to life? To your thoughts? No playing the victim or wearing rose-colored glasses. Just notice what's happening without judgement or blame. Be aware of it.

Can you see how all your life experiences, both positive and negative, have shaped who you are today? Can you hold conflicting viewpoints and emotions simultaneously? Can you let everything be what it is without forcing it into what you want it to be? Can you acknowledge your imperfections and forgive yourself for what you perceive as "bad"? Maybe your mistakes, and those of others, weren't actually mistakes, but rather lessons you weren't ready to see.

To do all this, we need to create mental, physical, and emotional space for self-reflection. We need stillness.

Pico Iyer, travel writer and author of *The Art of Stillness*, has discovered that Nowhere is his favorite place to visit. In this age of distraction, nothing is as urgent as stillness. When we sit still, we can find what moves us most and where our truest happiness lies. "So much of life takes place inside our heads, in memory or imagination or interpretation or speculation," he says, "that if I really want to change my life, I might best begin by changing my mind."

When I think of stillness, I'm reminded of the exact opposite: fidgeting in church as a kid, longing to be running around outside. Sitting still is hard, even (especially?) as an adult. We're surrounded by distractions that pull us into perpetual busyness. But in the quiet solitude of stillness, we're able to lift our own veils and begin to truly see.

Hitting pause. Being present. Bringing awareness to our actions. Reflecting on our past. This is how we connect with our internal world and begin to know ourselves.

When you're in the heat of the moment, patterns and emotions can drive your actions before your conscious mind has a chance to grasp what's happening. But during quiet reflection, you have the luxury of looking back at those moments from the outside looking in. That change of perspective gives you the ability to see things more objectively.

Meditations by Roman emperor and Stoic philosopher Marcus Aurelius is a written account of insights and advice to himself as he ruled over one of the greatest empires in history. He offers this endorsement of stillness: "People seek retreats for themselves in the country, by the sea, or in the mountains. You are very much in the habit of yearning for those same things. But this is entirely the trait of a base person, when you can, at any moment, find such a retreat in yourself. For nowhere can you find a more peaceful and less busy retreat than in your own soul—especially if on close inspection it is filled with ease, which I say is nothing more than being well-ordered. Treat yourself often to this retreat and be renewed."

This stillness is what I briefly experienced the night I attempted Ian's meditative exercise on forgiveness. Through stillness we can see with greater clarity how all of our choices have led us to where we are. In this stillness is the opportunity to greet our shadow selves, paving the way for empathy, compassion, and forgiveness.

The ego is all about "I," but our shadow is what connects us as human beings to wholeness. At some point in our lives, we all feel fear, guilt, shame, regret, worry, jealousy, disappointment, sadness, embarrassment, loneliness, pain, and anger. Those moments can feel isolating because we think our pain is unique to us. It's not. When we share our pain, we share our humanity.

When we open our eyes to the full spectrum of ourselves and others—the good and the bad—we can be gentler with each other. Gentleness is the root of compassion, which is the acknowledgement of our shared humanity.

If you recall from Chapter 4, this is also what happened when my wife and I practiced the mirroring exercises. We didn't see bad people. We saw similar patterns of protecting ourselves from more pain. Although we weren't consciously looking for forgiveness then, the other's compassion and understanding chipped away at the edges of our shame and fear, providing a sense of safety that paved the way to forgiveness for each other and ourselves. Not just for the "bad" things, but for everything. Forgiveness for each snowflake, not just the avalanches.

In the Lord's Prayer we ask God to "Forgive us our trespasses, as we forgive those who trespass against us." The only addition I'd make is to also "forgive ourselves our own trespasses." We are not so different from one another. Forgiveness *is* the path to integration of the shadow self and to a more harmonious world, a world where shadow and light dance together, embracing the ebbs and flows of life.

10

Harmony

When the world knows beauty as beauty, ugliness arises
When it knows good as good, evil arises
Thus, being and non-being produce each other
Difficult and easy bring about each other
Long and short reveal each other
High and low support each other
Music and voice harmonize each other
Front and back follow each other
Therefore, the sages:
Manage the work of detached actions
Conduct the teaching of no words
They work with myriad things but do not control
They create but do not possess
They act but do not presume
They succeed but do not dwell on success
It is because they do not dwell on success
That it never goes away

~ Tao Te Ching

The *Tao Te Ching* is an ancient Chinese text and one of the building blocks of Taoism. *Tao,* meaning "way," guides people to go with, not against, the flow of life. The goal is not to "be good" at all costs but rather to allow all of it, not pushing anything away. Only by acknowledging the duality of life, as well as our interdependence with nature, will we find harmony.

The Chinese yin and yang symbol represents this combining of two opposite yet interconnected forces. In its most simplistic form, yin symbolizes darkness and is associated with passive, feminine energy. Yang is light and is associated with active, masculine energy. Neither side is better than the other; both are needed to achieve harmony. In fact, the dot at the center of each side reminds us that there is always a piece of one within the other.

You can't have light without darkness, cold without heat, man without woman, fire without water, summer without winter, old without young, rich without poor, comfort without discomfort, order without chaos, good without bad.

Remember the *yetzer hara*, the evil inclination, from the second chapter? The other side of it is called the *yetzer hatov*, or good inclination. This rabbinic duality provides a Western perspective on the concept of yin and yang.

We spend much of our lives trying to stay on the side of goodness, but at what cost? And to what end?

Note the difference between harmony and balance. The goal of balance is equality—not too much of one thing or the other. If a scale tips too far in one direction, the balance is out of whack. Harmony, in contrast, is the integration of both or of multiple components, none necessarily in equal measures. We see this in nature, which regulates itself over time. There is an ease to harmony, whereas balance can feel forced.

While life may feel like a tennis match at times, with good and bad being whacked back and forth at a nauseating pace, it isn't a professional sport; it isn't about keeping score.

We can find harmony within ourselves by integrating the external messages we receive with our internal voice, the ego with the shadow, the goodness with the badness. It's not either/or; it's both. The goal isn't to be equally good and bad. It's to accept all parts of ourselves, without judgement, and bring them together to find our way.

Daily deep breathing exercises, consciousness meditation, professional therapy, and journaling are the tools I use to bring all the pieces of myself together. Over time my edges have softened, opening me up to greater empathy, compassion, kindness, and gratitude for everything and everyone around me. The world doesn't feel as tight and constricted. Quite the opposite, it feels vast and generous. Through my continued practice, the fuzziness of life has started to snap into focus.

Healing work is a lifelong commitment, however, and so I've come to cherish those moments when life's anxieties aren't weighing heavily on my chest. And rather than fearing their inevitable return, I stay firmly planted in the present. Okay, that's a bit of an exaggeration. I *try* to stay firmly planted in the present as much as possible. It takes conscious effort and awareness. A gentle vigilance: think Steve Jobs meets the Dalai Lama, if you will! When I can, I replace frustration in the healing process with reverence—knowing it can take just as long to wade out of the water as it does to wade in. You can't fast-track it.

What used to be an unknown mystical force pulling me toward something has become clearer and more deliberate. I don't actually know what that mystical force *is*, nor do I think I ever will, but I trust it more than ever. When I forfeited my scholarship, I had no idea why I did it. When I hitchhiked across the country, there was a stirring inside that I couldn't quite put my finger on. But when I moved from New York back to my home province of British Columbia and eventually put our family roots down on a farm, I knew why I did it.

On paper, it didn't make good sense. It wasn't the "right" decision. It wasn't "good" business. My business required me to be in the city. Our friends were in the city. Believe you me, many people were not shy about telling me I was crazy to start a farm. I'd heard it all before. Sure, I was a bit stressed and burnt out with the tolls of city life, but this time there wouldn't be any excuses or finger pointing. I *wanted* to go. It felt right (that mystical force in action!). As for the hypothetical problems and lost opportunities that might result? Well, I'd cross those bridges later.

I had taken my medicine journey a few years prior to our move, and since then I had maintained a fairly steady practice of meditation and journaling. That practice also included focused integration with my shadow self. I was just as committed to bringing the swamp-exploring dirtbag traveler back into my life as I was the champion runner.

The self-discovery and healing I experienced was nudging me closer to my whole self, which naturally forced me to reconcile the endless pace and progress of the city with the stillness and flow of living close to nature. Both were part of me. I saw the decision to move as a journey unto itself, one that likely started on the windswept plains of Canada's prairies when I hitchhiked across the country, an experience that gave me my first true taste of freedom to be my whole self. This feeling of living from my authentic self percolated while I pushed my mental and physical limits in the towering mountains of British Columbia, but it really coalesced when Ayahuasca opened up the corners of my mind. Our move wasn't a singular decision. It had been brewing for many years as I brought disparate parts of myself together, piece by piece.

Writing this now, the idea of living in harmony between two drastically opposed ways of life seems obvious, but back then I had a hard time figuring out how to make it work. External voices were saying "bad idea," yet everything I read corroborated what I instinctively knew and serendipitously saw unfolding in front of me.

Embracing the wild and primitive side of myself as a farmer allowed me to further open the door to other aspects of my shadow self. Curious to see what new life experiences might unfold, I didn't shut it.

As a slower work pace and increasing presence with my family emerged, I noticed other aspects of me start to unwind. I was less worried about—just about everything. And I started listening more intently to what was rattling around inside, allowing it to come out.

This wasn't purely the result of my inner work, although that was a big part of it. We now know that engaging in green microbreaks—taking time to look at nature through the window, on a walk outside, or even on a screensaver (although I recommend the natural version)—can be helpful for improving attention and performance in the workplace. Most of us already know this is something we can do, regardless of where we live or work.

As well, a concept called biophilic design–which incorporates natural elements into indoor environments–can help us recover from stress and anxiety more quickly and perform better cognitively. Simply adding plants to your space, incorporating natural materials like wood and bamboo, or decorating with images of nature can calm the mind and increase focus.

Perhaps all this is because we're less pixel and more dirt than we'd like to believe. Perhaps we are small pieces of a much larger, more natural whole. Nature reminds us of our interconnectedness by providing a counterbalance to the blue-light-emitting screens that demand our time and zap our energy. Nature is a dot of yin in our yang, grounding us with a sense of stillness and calm. And inversely, "the machine" is that contrasting dot in our natural selves.

To paraphrase the Roman Emperor and Stoic philosopher, Marcus Aurelius, he proposed you can punctuate your life with moments of stillness wherever you are. Psychiatrist Elisabeth Kübler-Ross reminds us of this: "Learn to get in touch with silence within yourself and know that everything in this life has a purpose. There are no mistakes, no coincidences; all events are blessings given to us to learn from. There is no need to go to India or anywhere else to find peace. You will find that deep place of silence right in your room, your garden or even your bathtub."

Honor your shadow by accepting the feelings that come with it: guilt, shame, envy, disappointment, loneliness, heartbreak, anger, unworthiness, and so forth. It is not sustainable to ignore your shadow because your bad informs your good; your meanness informs your kindness; your anger informs your forgiveness; your mistakes inform your growth; your wounds inform your healing; your failures inform your triumphs; your pain informs your compassion; your fears inform your freedom.

Embracing all of it allows you to drop the illusion that good and bad are separate from each other. In *The Art of War*, Sun Tzu says, "The greatest victory is that which requires no battle." Vanquish the desire to battle your badness.

What if all your negative feelings, anxiety, and perceived badness are an important precondition for feeling and experiencing something good?

If we lived only by the "good" *yetzer hatov*, there would be nothing to learn, and that is because there would be no challenges to grow from. As Rabbinic tradition teaches, the *yetzer hara* actually leads to a functioning society because commerce, community, marriage, and children wouldn't exist without the "evil" drives for sex, pleasure, and security.

The *yetzer hara* is essential to life, but it is not bad (just as the *hatov* is not good). They represent our inherent inclination toward both, which tugs at us as we go through life. How we respond to that tugging is our choice.

We can do something bad and still be a good person. We can cultivate compassion and forgiveness while slaying our own internal dragons. We can follow our internal guidance without completely tuning out society, religion, our parents, and other external voices. We can choose to remove the limitations that have been imposed on us—mostly by ourselves. That's harmony. That's maturity.

As clinical psychologist and author Jordan Peterson says, "You could be more than you are. And wouldn't that be great for everyone, including you."

Part of the impetus for writing this book was to inspire my daughters. If you've read this far, I'm sure you can tell I desperately want them to understand the importance of listening to their inner voice and of not looking at the world as a place of either/or. Rather, I want them to live without the limitations I felt constricted by for most of my life.

Now I understand that many of those limitations came from my environment and the events of my life. They were self-imposed limits, and they were perpetuated because I ignored my internal voice and clung so tightly to being good. When my shadow surfaced, I shoved it in the closet like a toy I had outgrown, hoping to never see it again.

I realize this desire to "heal the line" may very well have had the opposite effect. "Dad is just a self-help nutter who wants us to balance our good and bad," I can hear them saying. The irony of them healing the traumas I've inadvertently inflicted on them (this self-help agenda included) is not lost on me. I suppose that's a fear many parents harbor, that we'll unconsciously pass down our negative beliefs and unhealthy patterns, no matter how much healing we've done and how much effort we put into preventing such a bequeathal.

In reality, we can't protect our kids from all the external messages they receive or how they internalize those messages. We can't prevent those snowflakes from falling on them. But we can teach them how to trigger mini avalanches to prevent giant ones.

Even if you don't believe we all start out as blank slates, one look at a child acting out their vivid imagination in play might remind you what it's like not to care what other people think. What it's like to do something simply because you want to, because something inside is begging to come out.

According to Dr. Lisa Miller, author of *The Spiritual Child*: "A child's spirituality precedes and transcends language, culture, and religion. It comes as naturally to children as their fascination with a butterfly or a twinkling star-filled night sky. However, as parents we play a powerful role in our child's spiritual development, just as we play a powerful role in every other aspect of our child's development."

I might add, our children are also capable of slapping another child and of screaming at us when we refuse to give them candy, and yet still be little Zen Buddhas—blissfully unattached to any of it. Isn't that a beautiful expression of duality and harmony?

And all this is a reminder for me to be mindful of what I impart to them as their father. This poem by Kahlil Gibran expresses this sentiment beautifully.

Life's Longing for Itself

Your children are not your children.
They are sons and daughters of Life's longing for itself.
They come through you but not from you.
And though they are with you, yet they belong not to you.

You may give them your love but not your thoughts,
For they have their own thoughts.
You may house their bodies but not their souls,
For their souls dwell in the house of tomorrow,
which you cannot visit, not even in your dreams.
You may strive to be like them,
but seek not to make them like you.

For life goes not backward nor tarries with yesterday.
You are the bows from which your children
as living arrows are sent forth.
The Archer sees the mark upon the path of the infinite,
and He bends you with His might
that His arrows may go swift and far.
Let your bending in the Archer's hand be for gladness;
For even as He loves the arrow that flies,
so He also loves the bow that is stable.

What both Miller and Gibran say so eloquently, I'll say in my simple dad voice: I want them to know they have choices. I want them to be who they are, not what I may hope or wish for them.

And I want that freedom for you too.

11

Freedom

*Freedom is not worth having if it does not include
the freedom to make mistakes.*

~ Mahatma Gandhi

I've made several hard left turns in my life. Mistakes, some people would call
them. Maybe even bad choices. But those people don't get to judge what's
good and bad for me. All of my choices make up who I am, contributing to
the life I have now. And I love my life. The only limits that exist are the ones
I put on myself. To me, that is ultimate freedom.

We often judge others as a way to feel better about ourselves by thinking:
if he's bad, that makes me good, or at least better. But as the saying goes,
comparison is the death of joy. When we direct our energy to someone we
see as better off, it kills the good we experience in life and the good we see
in ourselves.

Striving to be a better version of ourselves is a worthy pursuit but, like I said
before, believing we're in competition with others suggests life is a zero-sum
game. I spent most of my childhood competing, unaware of what was really
driving me. Winning races meant I was "better" and therefore entitled to
what felt like scarce resources: love and acceptance.

When we see someone else succeeding and secretly wish they would fall on their face, we're buying into the idea that life is one giant pie, and that there are only so many slices of success. If someone else gets a slice, that means less for us.

Despite the way in which society pits us against each other (unrealistic standards of beauty, anyone?), the hand—or should I say mind?—that continuously condemns us is usually our own. When we feel inadequate, we look for someone less-than to reassure ourselves. But comparison never gives us what we ultimately want—to feel good enough.

Feeling worthy or deserving isn't in limited supply. You don't need to take it away from someone else to have it for yourself. Actually, you can't get it from someone else. It's an inside job that comes from accepting all parts of yourself.

You get to choose what you embrace and what you push away, what you hold onto and what you let go of. Just like this Buddhist story about two monks and a woman:

> Two monks were traveling together, one senior to the other. They came to a river with a strong current where a young woman was waiting, unable to cross alone. She asks the monks if they would help her across the river. Without a word, and in spite of the sacred vow he'd taken not to touch women, the older monk picks her up, crosses, and sets her down on the other side.
>
> The younger monk joins them across the river and is aghast that the older monk has broken his vow but doesn't say anything. An hour passes as they travel on. Then two hours. Then three. Finally, the agitated younger monk can no

longer stand it, so he asks, "Why did you carry that woman when we took a vow not to touch women?" The older monk replies, "I set her down hours ago by the side of the river. Why are you still carrying her?"

What are you still carrying? Can you let it go?

There is a children's story by Jack Kent called *There's No Such Thing as a Dragon.*

In the book, a boy wakes up to find a small dragon on the edge of his bed. With the innocence and honesty of a child, he tries to tell his parents that there is a dragon in the house, to which his always busy and preoccupied parents respond, "There is no such thing as a dragon." As the story progresses, and the boy's attempts to inform his parents about the dragon are in vain, the boy begins to ignore the dragon, too. Eventually, the dragon takes up the entire house, lifts it up, and moves it down the block. It's only then that the boy's parents notice the very big dragon. Their newfound awareness is the exact magic required to reverse the spell and bring the dragon back to a more manageable size, in this case, the size of a kitten.

When we ignore our problems, they become so large and detrimental that eventually they can no longer be ignored.

For a long time, I internalized my mother's desire for my success as bad thing, and the conversation about it that never happened became like the large dragon in the book.

Interestingly, though, as healing through shadow integration occurred in other, focused areas, its golden halo touched all corners of my shadow.

When my mother sat me down one day, tears in her eyes, to discuss that fateful night before the race and the pressure she'd put on me, surprisingly the conversation was free of any pain or resentment I had once so tightly harbored.

In fact, as my lovely mother sat there—as I'm sure I will one day sit there as a father of adult children, burning in the long-carried guilt from mistakes made in the past—I did not forgive her. I did not need to forgive her because I realized her good intentions. Her deep care. Her own shadow. She had done nothing wrong.

It was as spiritual teacher and Jesuit priest Anthony De Mello shares in his book *Awareness*, "In understanding, *it* disappears. The more you fight darkness the more real it becomes to you, the more you exhaust yourself. But when you turn on the light of awareness, it melts."

When I understood the root of what I was carrying, where it had come from, and why it was there for me and for my mother, it melted away. All the analysis of what was good and bad that resulted in these events of my life could no longer be labeled–they just were. They were the experiences that made me, me.

Although I, too, wept, they were not tears of sadness but tears of release that carried away the remains of the past lingering in my being.

We were both free of this now.

Blaming society or parents or circumstances is a way to stay stuck in your limited view of the world. When a voice tells you something is bad or wrong or not worth doing, find some stillness and challenge that voice. Ask where it's coming from. Is it the same old tune you've heard over and over, accepting it out of habit? Or is something deep inside telling you to go the other way?

Are "you" screaming from the shadows? Question all of it, listen to all of it, embrace all of it, feel the emotions that come up, then make a choice.

We know that some innate psychological forces are set against us: the brain's negativity bias, our desire for comfort, the primal need for safety and belonging. You can acknowledge these obstacles and decide to proceed anyway.

When your inner critic tells you you're not good enough or you're undeserving or you should just be happy with what you have, thank it for trying to keep you safe and forge ahead. You don't need to shut that voice out, but you don't need it to motivate you either.

When you get a glimpse of your shadow—maybe a burst of rage, shame, envy, or a desire to do something "bad"—don't push it away. Sit with it and accept it as part of you, but don't let it define who you are. You are darkness and light. The negative thoughts and desires you have are just part of being human. It goes against nature to try to live only within the light.

When I walked out the door of my childhood home to hit the highway, I unknowingly invited my emotions along for the ride. During those long stretches of roadside stillness, I sat in my shame, self-judgement, and unworthiness. Eventually, with a little help from counselors, friends, total strangers, my wife, children and, yes, Mother Aya, I connected those feelings to my real motivation for wanting to win races: to make myself worthy of love. I was able to see my "enoughness," not because I won races but because I was human. They saw the light in me, which helped me see it too.

Let me say it again: dark and light, success and failure, good and bad are two sides of the same coin—you can't have one without the other. Our old, familiar habit of keeping the shadow at bay feels safe, even if it makes us miserable. Our shadow is unpredictable and it's uncomfortable because we've made it unknown. But that so-called bad wolf can still be a loyal companion, and it might just help us carve out a beautifully full and rich life that's totally different from the one we *think* we want. The one we're told we *should* want.

When you see someone in your life ignoring the "shoulds" and breaking cultural rules, do you feel inspired or uncomfortable? Maybe a little of both? You can do it too. You can express your freedom by being your authentic self. When someone else does it, it shows you that your excuses are thin. But going against what you know and what you've always done can be downright terrifying. What if you take a big risk and it doesn't work out? What if everyone else is right and you're wrong?

You're not wrong.

You are but flesh, blood, and stardust existing in a vast universe that we don't fully understand.

You simply ARE.

Everything you need to make decisions about your life is available to you. A choice may not always be obvious, but deep inside you there is a knowing your mind doesn't want to acknowledge. Perhaps because it appears like a crazy and untrustworthy voice, like a rebellious child. Once again, listen anyway.

Dive into the abyss of discomfort. Challenge yourself physically, mentally, emotionally. Put a *misogi* on the calendar to push your limits so that you can see that most of your limits are self-imposed.

A beautiful example of this comes in the form of a story about Jace and the Iron Cowboy. Another running story, but this time it's not mine.

James Lawrence, known as the Iron Cowboy, is an endurance athlete who regularly does what others believe to be impossible. By breaking those boundaries of human endurance, he helps others rethink what they believe is possible for themselves.

He earned his nickname by completing one hundred Ironman races in one hundred days. That's one triathlon consisting of a 2.4-mile swim, a 112-mile bicycle ride, and a 26.2-mile marathon run per day for more than three months in a row. Ironman is considered one of the most challenging one-day sporting events in the world, and he did a hundred of them in a row with no days off. That's more than a little mind-blowing.

One of the many people James inspired was six-year-old Jace, who really wanted to run with the Iron Cowboy for a few miles during one of the Ironman races. So Jace's dad took him. After knocking out three miles, Jace's proud father halted their run and said, "Okay, we did it!" suggesting his son's wish had been fulfilled.

"But the Iron Cowboy is still going!" Jace replied, with tears in his eyes. Even though he had zero running experience, he had no quit in him and pushed through twenty miles that day. But Jace was devastated he didn't finish the race.

Some days later, Jace returned to run another leg with the Iron Cowboy, but this time he finished the entire marathon. He was absolutely elated. Unfortunately, Jace's father faced criticism for allowing his son to fight through the tears and the pain long-distance running brings—bad father! But the gift he gave his son was priceless—good father! And that gift? Limits are only what you believe them to be. With no limiting beliefs you are free to do whatever you believe is possible.

Nobody is all hero or all villain, and any attempt to confine someone (yourself included) to one of those boxes denies the dual nature of our existence and our ability to cultivate harmony within it. 'Tis true, we are mostly a confusing mess of seemingly opposite forces pulling us in different directions all the time. I say mostly because, though I've heard of people who are not, I just haven't met one yet. You can be envious of someone, yet still happy for them; you can be sad about an ending and excited about what comes next; you can find little pieces of joy even inside your pain. Instead of trying to force one or the other, true freedom, as well as true maturity, comes from finding harmony in both.

This is what I got wrong for so much of my life: I thought bad equaled unworthy. I thought that to deserve love, attention, and all the riches of the world, I had to be good. I conflated behavior with identity and thought it was all or nothing. If I "do" good that must mean I "am" good. There wasn't room in my worldview for good people doing bad things. Now I understand that's simply a fact of being human. We all have goodness and badness inside of us. Yin and yang.

To borrow wisdom from Bruce Tift in his book *Already Free*: "In my experience, what we discover when we are able to stay with both positive and negative experiences is that life is already supporting us. Actually, we find that it is our willingness to commit to all of our experience, regardless of our preferences, that supports us. It's very common that we feel that 'something's missing' from our lives. So, we search for love or security or enlightenment or whatever. But what's actually missing is our full participation in our ongoing, immediate experiencing. We are what's missing. When we are fully engaged in our life, regardless of whether we like or don't like what's present, we no longer have the drama of something missing."

Leaving school, hitchhiking, traveling the world, taking Ayahuasca—these were all attempts to find what was missing. By trying so hard to be good and only living within the light, I avoided my darkness. But it still weighed on me like an 80-pound rucksack. You can try to ignore your shadow, but it's always there.

Now when I look in the mirror, I see a whole person who has experienced success and failure, love and pain, comfort and suffering, shame and pride, happiness and sadness. I have inherent goodness and badness, and I have the freedom to choose my path at any given moment. My only limitation is me. I choose my own guardrails.

I once heard from a friend that happiness comes from defining values and morals and living according to them with impeccable integrity. I try to avoid quoting psychoanalysts to my daughters and instead prefer to lean on the classic novel *Anne of Avonlea* by Lucy Maud Montgomery to convey a similar sentiment to them:

> Anne: "I haven't lived up to my ideals."
>
> "None of us ever do," said Mrs. Allan with a sigh. "But then, Anne, you know what Lowell says, 'Not failure but low aim is a crime.' We must have ideals and try to live up to them, even if we never quite succeed. Life would be a sorry business without them. With them it's grand and great." Hold fast to your ideals, Anne."

But here's the rub, those ideals we put on ourselves of good and bad have a sneaky little habit of changing, if not all the time, then at least over time. They, too, are reflections of what we see in the mirror every today.

So how about we forget about all this bullshit about good and bad? I was a long-distance runner for many years, and I have reflected on my complicated relationship with running throughout the book, using it as an example of my struggle with good and bad. You have your own experiences, and I hope these pages have provided you with an opportunity to explore your beliefs about good and bad. Perhaps you'll challenge them, maybe even reframe them.

For this, I offer a poem by Hafiz called *A Golden Compass* as inspiration:

> Forget every idea of right and wrong any classroom ever taught you
>
> Because an empty heart, a tormented mind, unkindness, jealousy and fear
>
> Are always the testimony you have been completely fooled!
>
> Turn your back on those who would imprison your wondrous spirit
>
> With deceit and lies.
>
> Come, join the honest company of the King's beggars –
>
> Those gamblers, scoundrels and divine clowns and those astonishing fair courtesans
>
> Who need Divine Love every night.
>
> Come, join the courageous who have no choice but to bet their entire world
>
> That indeed, indeed, God is real.
>
> I will lead you into the circle of the Beloved's cunning thieves,

Those playful royal rogues, the ones you can trust for true
guidance –

Who can aid you in this blessed calamity of life.

Hafiz, look at the Perfect One at the circle's center:

He spins and whirls like a Golden Compass, beyond all
that is rational,

To show this dear world that everything, everything in
existence

Does point to God.

Give yourself permission to explore the parts of you that are good and the parts
that are bad. This doesn't mean engaging in harmful or destructive behaviors
but rather in accepting this duality as part of your nature. By integrating
your good and bad, ego and shadow into wholeness, there is no limit to what
you can do or the freedom you'll feel. Just remember that both the wolves
within are sacred animals and they both need your loving care.

Susan Cain poses important questions in her book *Bittersweet: How Sorrow
and Longing Makes Us Whole* that I hope *this* book has at least partially helped
you to answer. Cain's question is: "How do we get to the point of seeing our
sorrows and longings not as indications of secret unworthiness but as features
of humanity? How do we come to realize that embracing our inner loser as
well as winner—the bitter and the sweet—is the key to transcending them
both, the key to meaning, creativity, and joy?"

There is so much wisdom inside of you. Quiet yourself and listen to it. Trust it.

You don't need to dismiss the external voices or doctrines, but don't blindly live your life by them. Take all of it in, then make a choice. Again and again and again. That's the greatest gift you can give yourself and the world.

It has been so good to be with you through these pages. I may not know you, but I do know you are a beautiful expression of darkness and light. By bringing all pieces of yourself into wholeness, into conscious awareness, your self-imposed guardrails will disappear, and your inherent goodness will shine through. That is true freedom.

I'll close with Rumi: "Out beyond ideas of wrongdoing and rightdoing there is a field. I'll meet you there."

— THE END —

Bibliography

American Psychological Association. "Dichotomous Thinking." *APA Dictionary of Psychology*. Updated April 4, 2018. https://dictionary.apa.org/dichotomous-thinking.

Anwar, Yasmin. "How Many Different Human Emotions Are There?" *Greater Good Magazine,* September 8, 2017. https://greatergood.berkeley.edu/article/item/how_many_different_human_emotions_are_there.

Aurelius, Marcus. *Meditations*. Penguin, (180AD) 2019.

Avenanti, Alessio. "Emotions in Everyday Life." *PLoS One 10*, no. 12 (2015): e0145450. https://doi.org/10.1371/journal.pone.0145450.

Boyle, Gregory. *Forgive Everyone Everything.* Chicago: Loyola Press, 2022.

Brandt, Andrea. "Why Forgive? Because It's Good for You." *Psychology Today*, March 3, 2022. https://www.psychologytoday.com/us/blog/mindful-anger/202203/why-forgive-because-it-s-good-you.

Brown, Brené. "Shame vs. Guilt." *Brené Brown*, January 15, 2013. https://brenebrown.com/articles/2013/01/15/shame-v-guilt.

_____.The *Gifts of Imperfection: Let Go of Who You Think You're Supposed to Be and Embrace Who You Are.* Center City, MN: Hazelden, 2010.

Burgis, Luke. *Wanting: The Power of Mimetic Desire in Everyday Life.* New York: St. Martin's Press, 2021.

Campbell, Joseph. *The Hero with a Thousand Faces*. 3rd ed. Novato, CA.: New World Library, (1949) 2008.

Cain, Susan. *Bittersweet: How Sorrow and Longing Makes Us Whol*e. New York: Crown, 2023.

_____. *Quiet: The Power of Introverts in a World That Can't Stop Talking.* New York: Broadway Books, An Imprint Of The Crown Publishing Group, A Division Of Random House, Cop, 2013.

Carlton, Genevieve. "How History's Most Famous Extroverts Changed History." *Ranker,* September 27, 2018. https://www.ranker.com/list/extroverts-who-changed-history/genevieve-carlton.

Cherry, Kendra. "The 6 Types of Basic Emotions and Their Effect on Human Behavior." *Very Well Mind,* December 1, 2021. https://www.verywellmind. coman-overview-of-the-types-of-emotions-4163976.

_____. "What Is Negativity Bias?" *Very Well Mind,* November 13, 2023. https://www.verywellmind.com/negative-bias-4589618.

Christensen, Wendy. "Torches of Freedom: Women and Smoking Propaganda." *Society Pages,* February 27, 2012. https://thesocietypages.org/sociages/2012/02/27/torches-of-freedom-women-and-smoking-propaganda/.

Chödrön, Pema. *When Things Fall Apart: Heart Advice for Difficult Times.* 20th Anniversary ed. Boulder, CO: Shambhala, (1996) 2016.

Clear, James. *Atomic Habits: An Easy & Proven Way to Build Good Habits & Break Bad Ones.* New York, NY: Avery, 2018.

"Culture War." *Cambridge Dictionary.* https://dictionary.cambridge.org/us/dictionary/english/culture-war.

"Dichotomous thinking," APA Dictionary of Psychology. Updated April 4, 2018. https://dictionary.apa.org/dichotomous-thinking.

Easter, Michael. *The Comfort Crisis: Embrace Discomfort to Reclaim Your Wild, Happy, Healthy Self.* Rodale Books, 2021.

_____. "The First Rule of Misogi: Don't Die." *Huckberry* (blog), May 10, 2022. https://huckberry.com/journal/posts/michael-easter-misogi.

Easwaran, Eknath. *The Bhagavad Gita. Easwaran's Classics of Indian Spirituality Book 1.* Tomales, CA: Nilgiri Press, 2009.

Eisenstein, Charles. *The More Beautiful World Our Hearts Know Is Possible.* Berkeley, CA: North Atlantic Books, 2013.

"Epigenetics | Psychology Today." *Psychology Today*, 2019. https://www.psychology today.com/us/basics/epigenetics.

"Ethics Unwrapped." *Moral Relativism.* https://ethicsunwrapped.utexas.edu/glossary/moral-relativism.

Fischer, Brendan. "A Banana Republic Once Again?" *PR Watch*, December 27, 2010. https://www.prwatch.org/news/2010/12/9834/banana-republic-once-again.

Frankl, Victor. "Between Stimulus and Response There Is a Space. In That Space Is Our Power to Choose Our Response." *Quote Investigator*, February 18, 2018. https://quoteinvestigator.com/2018/02/18/response/,

"Gazing at Nature Makes You More Productive: An Interview with Kate Lee." *Harvard Business Review*, September 1, 2015. https://hbr.org/2015/09/gazing-at-nature-makes-you-more-productive.

Glawson, Michael. "How Sigmund Freud's Ideas Gave Rise to the Modern Advertising Industry." *Medium*, December 18, 2021. https://michaelglawson.medium.com/how-sigmund-freuds-ideas-gave-rise-to-the-entire-advertising-industry-36d409eab09d.

Gross, Terry. "Reluctant Psychonaut Michael Pollan Embraces 'New Science' of Psychedelics." (transcript of interview). *Fresh Air, NPR*, May 24, 2019. https://www.npr.org/2019/05/24/726085011/reluctant-psychonaut-michael-pollan-embraces-new-science-of-psychedelics.

Gustafson, Craig, and Lipton, Bruce, PhD. "The Jump From Cell Culture to Consciousness." *Integrative Medicine* (Encinitas) 16, no. 6 (2017): 44–50. https://www.ncbi.nlm.nih.gov/pmc/articles/PMC6438088/.

Hanson, Rick. *Hardwiring Happiness: The New Brain Science of Contentment, Calm, and Confidence.* New York: Harmony, 2016.

Heinberg, Richard. *Memories and Visions of Paradise: Exploring the Universal Myth of a Lost Golden Age.* Los Angeles: Tarcher, 1990.

Henriques, Martha. "Can the Legacy of Trauma Be Passed down the Generations?" Bbc.com. *BBC Future,* March 26, 2019. https://www.bbc.com/future/article/20190326-what-is-epigenetics.

Homeboy Industries. "Transformation Story: Meet Jorge Dominguez." *Homeboy Industries.* https://homeboyindustries.org/transformation_story/jorge-dominguez/.

Iyer, Pico. "The Art of Stillness." TED*Salon,* August 2014. Video, 15:28. https://www.ted.com/talks/pico_iyer_the_art_of_stillness.

Jesse, Robert. "Entheogens: A Brief History of Their Spiritual Use." *Tricycle,* Fall 1996. https://tricycle.org/magazine/entheogens-a-brief-history-their-spiritual-use/.

Jobs, Steve. "How to Live before You Die." *Stanford,* October 6, 2011. Video, 15:04. https://www.ted.com/talks/steve_jobs_how_to_live_before_you_die?delay=5s.

———. "Steve Jobs Commencement Address at Stanford 2005 (Excerpt)." https://academyatthelakes.org/wp-content/uploads/2016/02/SteveJobsatStanfordUniversityExcerpts.pdf.

Jung, Carl. *Psychology and Religion.* New Haven, CT: Yale University Press, 1938.

Kahneman, Daniel. *Thinking, Fast and Slow.* New York: Farrar, Straus and Giroux, 2013.

LaBianca, Juliana. "10 Inspiring Stories of Extreme Forgiveness That Will Lift Your Spirits." *Inspiring Stories* (blog). *Reader's Digest,* June 14, 2022. https://www.rd.com/list/inspiring-forgiveness-stories/.

Li, Yuanyuan. "Modern Epigenetics Methods in Biological Research." *Methods* 187, July 2020. https://doi.org/10.1016/j.ymeth.2020.06.022.

Lieberman, Matthew D., Naomi I. Eisenberger, Molly J. Crockett, Sabrina M. Tom, Jennifer H. Pfeifer, and Baldwin M. Way. "Putting Feelings Into Words." *Psychological Science* 18, no. 5 (2007): 421-428. https://static1.squarespace.com/static/651b09f505bc433349d85ab7/t/651e4049a3f0a647cdf2ef0/1696481356642/Lieberman%2C_Psychological+Science%282007%29.pdf.

Maio, Gregory R. "Mental Representations of Social Values." *Advances in Experimental Social Psychology, Vol. 42*, edited by Mark P. Zanna, 1-43. Academic Press, 2010. https://www.sciencedirect.com/science/article/abs/pii/S0065260110420018.

Maden, Jack. "John Locke's Empiricism: Why We Are All Tabula Rasas (Blank Slates)." *Philosophy Break,* March 2021. https://philosophybreak.com/articles/john-lockes-empiricism-why-we-are-all-tabula-rasas-blank-slates/.

Macnamara, Deborah, and Gordon Neufield. *Rest, Play, Grow: Making Sense of Preschoolers (or Anyone Who Acts like One).* Vancouver: Aona Books, 2016.

Mcadams, Dan, and Kate C. McLean. "Narrative Identity." *Current Directions in Psychological Science* 22, no. 3 (2013): 233-238. https://www.researchgate.net/publication/269603657_Narrative_Identity.

Miller, Lisa. *The Spiritual Child.* New York: St. Martin's Press, 2015. https://www.cbc.ca/radio/tapestry/excerpt-from-the-spiritual-child-by-dr-lisa miller-1.3361911.

Miller, Michael Craig. "Unconscious or Subconscious?" *Harvard Health Blog*, Harvard Medical School, August 2, 2010. https://www.health.harvard.edu/blog/unconscious-or-subconscious-20100801255.

Montgomery, Lucy Maud. *Anne of Avonlea.* Seal Books, May 1, 1984.

Oppenheimer, Billy. "Skin Thickness, Rick Rubin, Act Before You Think, Mouth Taping, Getting Lucky With The Weather, and Why It's Better To Travel Than To Arrive," *Six and 6* (blog), February 6, 2022. https://billyoppenheimer.com/february-6-2022/.

Pasricha, Neil. *You are Awesome.* Simon & Schuster, November 5, 2019.

Perna, Mark C. "Not Your Parents' Career—Or Is It? Parents Exert Significant Influence On Kids' Career Choices." *Forbes,* November 16, 2021. https://www.forbes.com/sites/markcperna/2021/11/16/not-your-parents-career-or-is-it-parents-exert-significant-influence-on-kids-career-choices/?sh=324d88a3c1c9.

Pinker, Steven. "The Blank Slate." *New York Times,* October 13, 2002.

Rollin, Jennifer. "3 Reasons to Let Yourself Feel Your Emotions." *Psychology Today*, 2016. https://www.psychologytoday.com/us/blog/mindful-musings/201611/3-reasons-let-yourself-feel-your-emotions.

Seltzer, Leon F. "Subconscious vs. Unconscious: How to Tell the Difference." *Psychology Today*, December 4, 2019. https://www.psychologytoday.com/us/blog/evolution-the-self/201912/subconscious-vs-unconscious-how-tell-the-difference.

"SHADOW INTEGRATION 101." *The Lovett Center*, April 3, 2019. https://the lovettcenter.com/shadow-integration-101/.

Sun Tzu. *The Art of War*. Sun Tzu. 400BC.

Szegedy-Maszak, Marianne. "The Secret Mind - How Your Unconscious Really Shapes Your Decisions." *U.S. News & World Report*, February 28, 2005. https://hypnosis.edu/articles/secret-mind.

ThemeGrill. "What Is Mimetic Theory?" Violenceandreligion.com. January 24, 2017. https://violenceandreligion.com/mimetic-theory/.

Tracy, Brian. "The Power of Your Subconscious Mind | Brian Tracy." *Brian Tracy's Self Improvement & Professional Development Blog*, December 12, 2018. https://www.briantracy.com/blog/personal-success/understanding-your-subconscious-mind/.

Tift, Bruce. *Already Free: Buddhism Meets Psychotherapy on the Path of Liberation*. Boulder, CO: Sounds True, 2015.

Vaish, Amrisha, and Grossmann, Tobias, and Woodward, Amanda. "Not all emotions are created equal: The negativity bias in social-emotional development." Psychol Bulletin 134, no. 3 (2008): 383–403, https://doi.org/10.1037/0033-2909.134.3.383

van der Kolk, Bessel. *The Body Keeps the Score: Brain, Mind, and Body in the Healing of Trauma*. London: Penguin Books, 2015.

Warner, Judith. "Introduction," in *And Then They Stopped Talking to Me: Making Sense of Middle School*. New York: Crown, 2020, xxiii.

"What Is Transference?" WebMD, June 27, 2021. https://www.webmd.com/mental-health/what-is-transference.

World Population Review. "Religion by Country 2024." *World Population Review*, 2024. https://worldpopulationreview.com/country-rankings/religion-by-country.

Yin, Jie, Jing Yuan, Nastaran Arfaei, Paul J. Catalano, Joseph G. Allen, and John D. Spengler. "Effects of Biophilic Indoor Environment on Stress and Anxiety Recovery: A Between-Subjects Experiment in Virtual Reality." *Environment International* 136 (0160-4120): 105427. 2020. https://doi.org/10.1016/j.envint.2019.105427.

About The Author

An entrepreneur among other things, Joel Primus is the co-founder and creative visionary behind Naked Revival. Currently, Joel hosts The Ramble Podcast, where he has unbound and uncensored conversations about people, places, pursuits and performances. He is the director and producer of multiple documentaries and docuseries, including the award winning *Raising Global Citizens*, *Finding Nowhere*, *Colombia* and *Revive*, as well as the author of *Getting Naked: The Bare Necessities of Entrepreneurship and Startups*. He shares his thoughts and adventures on the joelprimus.com blog.

Once an elite long-distance runner, he now enjoys daily training, meditation, and time with his family on their farm outside Vancouver.

Other Works By Joel Primus

*Getting Naked: The Bare Necessities of Entrepreneurship and Start Up*s

Do you want to be an entrepreneur? Are you serious about starting a business? Joel Primus will show you how. From the small country town of Abbotsford to the skyscrapers of New York, this book shares the hard-learned lessons and captivating story of a start-up, Naked Boxer Briefs, a Nasdaq publicly traded company that had A-list celebrity endorsements, raised over 17 million dollars and sold its product in department stores around the world, including Nordstrom's and Bloomingdales.

Part memoir and part entrepreneur's start-up manual, *Getting Naked* reveals when and how to start your business, how to raise money, how to build teams and hire employees, and how to develop a solid brand, objective-based operations and marketing. Just as important, it also delves into the personal sacrifices required of an entrepreneur, exploring the vital links between mental health, family, finding balance and being true to you who are through it all.

The life of an entrepreneur is an uphill road with obstacles, sharp turns and hazardous road conditions. It's all too easy to lose both yourself and your business along the way. *Getting Naked* is your personal road map to business and personal success.

To enjoy this and other projects by the author visit *www.joelprimus.com* or contact *hello@joelprimus.com*.

Milton Keynes UK
Ingram Content Group UK Ltd.
UKHW020350211124
451507UK00012B/189/J

9 781068 889127